# The Lotus and the Artichoke
## Vegan Recipes from World Adventures

### Justin P. Moore

**The Lotus and the Artichoke**
**Vegan Recipes from World Adventures**
© 2012/2021 Justin P. Moore

The information in this book is true and complete to the best of my knowledge. This book is intended only as an informal guide for those wishing to know more about food, travel, and health issues. In no way is this book intended to replace, countermand, or conflict with advice given to you by a physician. Likewise, caution and common sense should be used in selecting travel destinations and activities. The information in this book is general and offered without any guarantee on the part of the author and publisher. The author and publisher disclaim all liability in connection with the use of this book.

**WORLD 2.0 English edition November 2021**
First English edition printed in December 2012

Design, Illustration & Photography: © Justin P. Moore

Printing & Binding: Buchdruck Zentrum

© for this edition Ventil Verlag UG (haftungsbeschränkt) & Co. KG
Edition Kochen ohne Knochen

**ISBN 978-3-95575-012-1**

Ventil Verlag
Boppstr. 25
55118 Mainz
Germany
**www.ventil-verlag.de**

**www.lotusartichoke.com**
facebook.com @lotusartichoke
instagram.com @lotusartichoke

THE LOTUS AND THE ARTICHOKE

VEGAN RECIPES FROM WORLD ADVENTURES

TVIA
ND
H REPUBLIC RUSSIA
TRIA HUNGARY
SLOVAKIA
TZERLAND
BIA
TENEGRO

TURKEY

ISRAEL

YPT QATAR

ETHIOPIA

KENYA

TANZANIA

CHINA

JAPAN

NEPAL MYANMAR
LAOS
INDIA CAMBODIA
VIETNAM

THAILAND

SRI LANKA MALAYSIA
SINGAPORE

(HAWAI'I)

GUAM MARSHALL
ISLANDS

MICRONESIA
~ETC.

## AFRICA

## EUROPE

# About this Cookbook

**The Lotus and the Artichoke - Vegan Recipes from World Adventures** was first published in 2012. In the years since, I've been to many more countries, met countless incredible individuals, made and shared thousands of meals in kitchens all over, and created a series of cookbooks inspired by my journeys and dedicated to the fantastic cuisines of **México** (2014), **Sri Lanka** (2015), **Malaysia** (2016), **India** (2017), and **Ethiopia** (2019).

In early 2020, I planned to return to Japan and continue my adventures and research from the previous year. But the pandemic struck and changed everything. The lockdowns and border closures meant drastic changes not just to daily life, work, and school – but to our travel aspirations as well. It became clear that my culinary and creative projects – and my priorities – would be staying very close to home. As life became more routine and restricted, I sought escape and comfort in the kitchen and my studio, revisiting the intense dishes, unforgettable places, and global flavors that have shaped my life and projects in the last nine years.

I've always attempted to make the most of obstacles and the unexpected. I embraced the challenges of these strange times and got to work recreating my classic first book. It was something I'd hoped to do for years – ever since the sequels came out, each more passionate, detailed, and refined than the last. After an intense year (full of unpredictability, domestic duties, homeschooling, struggles with focus, anxiety, and the bane of artistic perfectionism), this new edition of my original bestselling cookbook has finally emerged!

**This is WORLD 2.0 – the fully-revised and updated, deliciously re-photographed, freshly illustrated, expanded version of my original vegan cookbook!** It's got more stories, new and improved recipes, better photos, and more experience – with more attention to 'authenticity' and cultural context. From cover to cover it's a new book with upgraded visuals, clarity, and content – and more fun, flavor, and feeling than ever.

Just in case you're new to my books, let's back up and I'll tell you my story:
**The Lotus and the Artichoke** combines my lifelong passions – travel, cooking, art, photography, and design.

My family moved from the United States to the Marshall Islands, in the North Pacific, when I was five. From an early age, I was exposed to long journeys, world cultures, and parts of the globe with varied weather, scenery, tastes, and traditions. We took annual trips back to the US and often went on extended road trips and excursions to see friends, relatives, and national parks. In the winter, we toured other parts of Micronesia and Polynesia, vacationed in thatched huts and other accommodations, swam in tropical waters, explored island ruins and tropical jungles, and engaged with indigenous folk and local communities.

Our family had a strong tradition of healthy, explorative, and versatile eating. All of us were encouraged to cook. My three younger brothers and I often shared cooking duties with my mom during the week. Dad took the helm on the weekends and made us pancakes, waffles, and French toast. We experienced a variety of cuisines owing to our immigrant ancestors, including Russian-Ukrainian, German, and Polish dishes – especially when visiting my grandparents. We also enjoyed American classics and plenty of comfort food – baked casseroles, pasta, homemade pizza, and lots of fresh vegetables – ideally from our backyard garden or local farmer's markets. When we lived overseas, we got excited about Chinese and Japanese restaurants in Honolulu.

My early experiences with Thai, Mexican, and Ethiopian food were also with my family. At childhood friends' homes, I often snuck into the kitchen to peek in the fridge and pantry. I marveled at imported spices, bottled sauces and condiments, jars of kimchi or chilies, packages of udon noodles and soybean curd – so many specialities in packages with fascinating, foreign scripts and emblems. My love affair with Indian food began when I was only two years old – a friend of the family often took care of me and stuffed me with home-cooked curries and decadent sweets, forever defining my culinary tastes and desires.

I didn't go to culinary school, but I've always loved kitchens. I never aspired to be a chef, nor have my own restaurant. You see, I'm not really an expert or authority on cooking and culinary wisdom – I'm just a guy who has spent his life enjoying food and world cultures, living boldly, and hoping to give back some of the insight and wonder that have been shared with me. I love cooking for others and comparing recipes and ideas. I've learnt from watching, asking questions, lots of experimentation, practice, and willingness to make mistakes. I adore the challenge of recreating dishes, refining skills, exploring new ingredients, and I absolutely love to connect with people through food. Food has always been a dominant factor in my travel destinations.

Ever since I was a kid, I've been documenting my life, travels, visions, and ideas with artwork and photography. I knew from an early age that I wanted to be an artist, like my maternal grandmother. At thirteen, I'd gotten my first real camera and learned how to work in the darkroom to develop film and print photographs. After high school, I went on to study painting and printmaking. After completing a degree in Fine Arts, I moved to Boston and worked as a web programmer and designer. But after a few trips to Europe, a cross-country motorcycle adventure, jaunts to Canada and Mexico, and a couple visits to Asia and Africa, I was hungry for more.

So I left Boston and my career in interactive design and spent four months backpacking in India and Nepal, riding ramshackle trains and buses, trekking in the Himalayas, staying in ashrams and cheap guesthouses, all the while sharing meals, moments, laughter, and mishaps with locals and other travelers.

In 2001, I booked a one-way ticket to Berlin and moved to Germany. I immersed myself in learning German and connected with the international art scene. Between projects, I ventured around Europe and made my way to North Africa and back to Asia. For several years, I was the art director, lead designer, and cartographer for a walking tour company with outposts in fourteen cities. I met many amazing people, photographed lots of landmarks, and illustrated a lot of maps.

On an overnight train in South India in 2010, I met a young man searching for an Art and English teacher for an international school. A few months later, I'd subletted my apartment in Prenzlauer Berg and moved to India. I lived for a year in Amravati, Maharashtra. I ate and cooked constantly with neighbors and new friends.

Upon returning to Berlin, I nearly accepted a position at a school to continue teaching art. But I couldn't stop thinking about my travels, the food and cooking sessions in India, and how I'd always wanted to make a cookbook. I learned about crowdfunding and was introduced to Kickstarter. I dedicated the next six months to my dream.

I wrote, photographed, illustrated, and designed the first edition of **The Lotus and the Artichoke – Vegan Recipes from World Adventures**. I self-published a thousand copies with the help of hundreds of supporters around the world. The books were delivered to my doorstep in early December. I spent the next weeks signing and packing cookbooks – and going to the post office. Just before the first printing sold out a few months later, an independent publisher contacted me. They offered to publish a German edition and reprint the book in English. Since then, we've reprinted my first book many times and released English and German versions of another five cookbooks based on my culinary adventures.

I've toured Germany and other countries in Europe, hosted dinner parties and cooking classes, and done cooking shows at events, festivals, and conventions. Sometimes it even feels like I know what I'm doing!

Of course, there's another important aspect to all of this:

When I was 15, I decided to embrace a vegetarian way of life – for ethical, environmental, and health reasons. As early as eight, I'd made the connection between living animals and the food on our plates. It troubled me – eating animals didn't feel right or necessary. It seemed the only reason it persisted was because of tradition and taste, ignoring the suffering and waste.

When I was a bit older, I met a few vegetarians and read about the ethics, impact, economics, and politics of animal agriculture. I was inspired by musicians, writers, and others and I was reassured to discover that significant parts of the world population adhered to more compassionate, sensible, and sustainable ways of eating. By time I was seventeen, I'd transitioned to a vegan diet – in a time when the term was mostly unknown. Over the years, my eating habits – and culinary skills – have constantly evolved.

I've faced many challenges while on the road, but I've always strived to maintain my ideals and yet still express modesty, respect, and gratitude. The social aspects of food are woven undeniably deeply into our cultures. Whether we are at home with family, or elsewhere as a guest, we make choices which affect the health and welfare of ourselves, others, and our planet. Each of us must follow the path we believe to be right, to the extent possible and practicable. This is what has worked for me for nearly thirty years.

With this book – these recipes, pictures, and personal stories – I wish to share with you the appreciation and enjoyment I have gathered from my adventures in the unique countries and cultures that have hosted me, and all of the unforgettable meals and individuals that have inspired and guided me.

**Justin P. Moore**
September 2021
Berlin, Germany

# In the Kitchen

**These recipes use ingredients and cooking methods which are practical almost anywhere in world.**
Most conventional and organic supermarkets and grocery stores will have almost everything you'll need. Many ingredients you can find in the international sections of supermarkets, and at Asian & African markets and shops. Local markets are great for getting seasonal, fresh, organic produce.

I keep recipes as traditional as possible, but also provide suggestions for substitutions. I use few "exotic" ingredients, and typically provide alternatives. Experiment with new methods and ingredients – seek them out. Try not to omit or substitute, especially seasonings and key ingredients– unless you really must, or desire a different dish and taste. Often just a few ingredients make a huge difference in the taste, intensity, and wonder of meals.

Culinary exploration, experimentation, and exchange are fantastic things – I encourage them to be done with openness, awareness, and enjoyment. Authenticity is complex. Accuracy is always arguable. I try to regard the specifics and context from which culinary traditions and dishes originate. With respect, it's acceptable for you to make adaptations to suit tastes and availability.

My recipes are inspired by extensive research and sessions with cooks, friends, and family around the world. I seek to recreate and reflect the wonder that has been shared with me. I encourage you to explore and discover deeper for yourself.

## Following Recipes

Recipe descriptions and instructions are written as simply and clear as possible. My photographs give an idea of how your creation may turn out, and how to present it. Don't be upset if your dish looks different. My recipes are not exact formulas for perfection. They are meant as guidelines and inspiration. Stray from the recipes if you want (or need) to use more or less of particular ingredients.

If you're new to cooking and/or particular cuisines, ingredients, or methods: Follow recipes closely the first time to learn the basics, then explore. In my early years of cooking, I focused too much on creativity and improvisation – I made lots of mistakes and overlooked many fundamentals.

Portion estimates give you an idea of the recipe's yield. Most recipes are intended for 2 to 3 servings, others provide for 4 or more. My portions run small as many dishes – especially Asian – are intended to be served along with others. Keep this in mind if you're cooking only one dish for more than two people. Most recipes can be scaled up or down e.g. doubled or halved. Beyond that, you may need to adjust amounts and times.

Mise en place is the best: always prep your mind, workspace, tools, and ingredients first. Read through the recipe. Find and sort everything you need, including measuring, chopping, and slicing. Get ready and go!

Estimated cooking times do not include prep and idle time (soaking, rising, cooling, chilling, etc.) and are usually more true for the second or third time making a dish – once you're familiar with the flow. Recipes that involve idle time are marked with +.

Oven temperatures and times will vary depending on your oven. I recommend using an oven thermometer. Whether cooking on the stove or in the oven, I try to provide visual cues to guide you, not just cooking times.

## Weights & Measurements

My recipes use a combination of American and metric measurements. When creating recipes, I always measure both. I do not use standardized weights for various sizes of things – Vegetables and other items are weighed and recorded every time I write a recipe. Metric weights are far more accurate and reliable than volume amounts for recreating results: Your cup of flour or sugar might weigh 20–30% more or less than mine!

I recommend using a digital kitchen scale.

## Vegetables & Fruit

Always use fresh and organic ingredients whenever possible. You can still get excellent results with quality frozen ingredients, particularly peas, spinach, okra, and mango. Weights will vary because of the water content, and you'll need to thaw items and/or adjust cooking times. Canned/tinned items will often work fine, such as tomatoes and pineapples, but I prefer fresh for maximum flavor.

## Spices & Herbs

Grinding your own spices just before you use them will seriously upgrade the flavors of your cooking. Cumin, coriander seeds, and black pepper are three spices I always grind regularly. Grinding is also great for making your own spice mixes, but quality Garam Masala, Sambar Masala, Berbere, and Ras el Hanout from shops are fun and tasty. I do not recommend "curry powder", nor garlic powder or onion powder. Whenever possible, obtain spices from specialty (import) shops. Always keep spices well-sealed in a dry place away from heat and light, and replace them after a few months. Please. Old spices taste dull and ruin dishes!

Fresh herbs are vital to flavor. My favorites are coriander/cilantro, parsley, mint, and basil – they must be fresh. Dried rosemary, thyme, sage, dill, and Herbes de Provence are decent, but fresh always wins. Grow some! If you can get fresh curry and fenugreek leaves, definitely do! Otherwise, dried leaves work and are far easier to find. For store-bought minced garlic or ginger, 1 tsp is roughly equivalent to 1 clove or 1/2 in (1 cm) fresh.

I often avoid garlic and onions, as they often overpower more subtle flavors in many dishes. Consequently, many recipes feature a "vedic" variation rooted in Indian Ayurvedic tradition. Asafoetida (hing) and dried curry leaves are cheap and commonly available. Both are game changers for South Asian cuisines!

## Lentils & Beans

I often prefer soaking and cooking dried legumes instead of cooked, canned/tinned beans and lentils. Soak dried beans overnight, or cover them with boiling water and soak for a few hours. Rinse and cook them in fresh water – without salt (or they'll cook forever). Drain and rinse canned/tinned products before use.

## Flours & Grains

I recommend all-purpose (type 550) unbleached flour for most recipes. Blend up to half the quantity with whole grain flour for more nutrition and earthy feels. Spelt flour can usually be used with similar results. For all substitutions adjust liquid and salt amounts accordingly.

I recommend chickpea flour (Indian "besan" or "gram flour") and rice flour from Asian shops, as they are typically more finely ground and have better flavor than conventional and especially organic brands. Otherwise, you'll need to adjust (decrease) liquid amounts in recipes.

Corn starch/flour and tapioca starch/flour are featured in many recipes. Be careful with measurements and substitutions, especially with other binders which may have very different textures and binding strength!

Buy quality rice, especially basmati and sushi rice. Your dishes deserve it. Always rinse rice before steaming. Soak it, too – if you have time.

## Soy, Seitan, Meat Substitutes

I prefer organic extra firm tofu. Remove moisture excess moisture by cutting tofu in slabs, wrapping it in a dish towel, and applying weight (e.g. cutting boards) for 20–30 min. This helps the tofu soak up flavors and improves the texture. Some recipes use soft or silken tofu. Tofu can be substituted for seitan or soy meats in many recipes. Smoked tofu is a decent sub for Tofu Paneer (in Indian recipes) if you're in a hurry. Tempeh, especially smoked and seasoned, can be a versatile substitution for many dishes, too.

Soy mince and chunks (TVP) should be soaked in hot water or broth and then pressed to remove moisture. Larger pieces can be chopped or ripped. Frying them prior to adding liquid improves texture.

Seitan in a can from Asian shops is my favorite, but conventional and organic seitan from other stores is fine. Drain and rinse before use. Making and seasoning your own seitan can be fun, too.

My recipes do not use many processed meat substitutes, but products available these days are astounding. Experiment with your favorites in curries, stews, casseroles, quiches and more. Jackfruit, mushrooms, cauliflower, and potatoes are also substitution possibilities for many recipes.

## Sweeteners & Salt

For most recipes, I use organic, unrefined (raw) sugar or agave syrup. I avoid most refined sweeteners, but occasionally use powdered sugar or brown sugar. In dishes with citrus and sour ingredients, including lemon/lime juice, vinegar, or tamarind, I usually add sweetness to balance flavors.

I prefer sea salt and Himalayan (pink) salt, but also use regular iodized salt. Use what you prefer. Kala namak (black salt) is available at Asian shops. It a provides a rich, sulfur/egg flavor – just don't overdo it!

## Oil & Vinegar

When recipes call for vegetable oil, I recommend a neutral-tasting oil such as canola/rapeseed. Safflower is also okay, but I avoid sunflower and peanut oil because of their stronger flavors. I use extra virgin olive oil in many recipes. Get the quality that suits your budget. I also cook with quality, refined coconut oil and decent sesame oil. For margarine, I recommend Alsan, Naturli, Earth Balance, or other quality vegan spreads.

If reducing (or omitting) oil in recipes, be sure to lightly fry (or roast) spices early in cooking. Especially for Indian dishes, many spices do not stew or steam well, unless they've been pre-roasted or fried to activate flavors. Expect different results.

## Kitchen Tools & Cookware

Over the years and around the world, I've worked in all kinds of kitchens. It's amazing what can be done with even the most minimal arrangements – but there are indeed items and tools which will significantly upgrade your experience and results. Work with what you've got and appreciate whatever you can afford!

I recommend investing in a good, high-speed blender. I use mine every day for sauces, soups, milks, creams, smoothies, and desserts. (My recipes have been tested with and are possible with inexpensive blenders, too.)

A small food processor, or personal blender, is great for smaller amounts and blending pastes. Immersion blenders are helpful for soups or mashed potatoes, but I don't use one for much else.

An electric coffee/spice grinder is awesome for grinding spices, nuts, and seeds. I also use an old-fashioned heavy-duty mortar and pestle. Asian rice cookers are excellent for superior rice, every time.

I use a collection of stainless steel pots, and a set of high-quality non-stick pots and pans, all with decent, fitting lids. A well-seasoned cast-iron wok and crêpe pan are fantastic, too.

I only have a couple of semi-fancy knives, nothing especially expensive. It works for me!

## Kitchen Inventory & Ingredients Master List:

### Tools
knives (small, large, serrated)
kitchen scale (digital)
measuring cups & spoons
mixing bowls (small, medium, large)
cutting boards (small, medium, large)
colander
lemon & lime squeezer/press
mortar & pestle
pastry brush (silicone)
sieve/strainer (metal/mesh)
serving spoons / ladles
slotted spoons (metal)
wooden spoons
spatula
vegetable grater
vegetable peeler
whisks (small, medium)
zester / Microplane

### Cookware
crêpe pan (seasoned cast-iron)
frying/sauce pans (small, medium, large)
pots (small, medium, large – with lids)
pressure cooker
wok (non-stick or seasoned cast-iron)

### Bakeware
baking tray (metal, non-stick)
baking/casserole dish (round, rectangular)
muffin pan/bakeform
springform pan/bakeform

### Kitchen Appliances
high-powered blender
small food processor
immersion blender
spice/coffee grinder (electric)
rice cooker

## Spices & Seasonings (dried)
allspice
amchoor (mango) powder
asafoetida (hing)
bay leaves
Berbere spice mix
black pepper (whole, ground)
cardamon (whole, ground)
cinnamon (sticks, ground)
cloves (whole)
coriander seeds (whole, ground)
cumin (whole, ground)
curry leaves
fenugreek leaves (kasuri methi)
Garam Masala (spice mix)
Herbes de Provence
juniper berries
kala namak (black salt)
mustard seeds (black/brown)
nutmeg (whole, ground)
paprika (ground)
Ras el Hanout (spice mix)
saffron (threads, ground)
Sambar Masala (spice mix)
sea salt
turmeric (ground)

## Fresh Herbs
basil
coriander/cilantro
curry leaves
dill
mint
oregano
parsley
rosemary
sage
thyme

## Nuts & Seeds
almonds
brazil nuts
cashews
chia seeds
flax seeds
hazelnuts
hemp seeds
peanuts
sesame seeds (white, black)
sunflower seeds
walnuts

## Dried Fruit
apricots
cranberries
dates
figs
plums (prunes)
raisins

## Beans & Lentils
black beans
brown lentils
chickpeas (garbanzo beans)
kidney beans
northern/white beans
red lentils
toor dal
urid dal (split, hulled & whole)

## Grains
arborio (risotto) rice
basmati rice
brown rice
bulgur
couscous
jasmine rice
lasagna noodles
mee (thin wheat noodles)
oats (steel-cut, rolled)
pasta (macaroni, spaghetti, etc)
rice noodles
quinoa
semolina
sushi rice

## Flours
all-purpose flour (type 550)
chickpea flour (besan)
corn starch/flour
rice flour
soy flour
spelt flour
tapioca starch/flour
whole wheat flour

## Oils
coconut oil
margarine (Alsan, Earth Balance)
olive oil (extra virgin)
sesame oil
vegetable oil (canola/rapeseed)

## Vinegar & Wine
apple cider vinegar
balsamic vinegar
rice vinegar
red wine vinegar
red wine
white wine

## Sweeteners
agave syrup
blackstrap molasses
brown sugar
jam/marmalade
maple syrup
powdered sugar
unrefined (raw) sugar

## Other
alfalfa seeds (for sprouting)
baking powder
baking soda
cocoa powder (unsweetened)
coconut (grated)
coconut milk (min. 60%)
peanut butter
hot sauce / chili sauce
lemon juice
lime juice
nutritional yeast flakes
oat milk
soy sauce (shoyu or tamari)
soy milk
soy cream
tahini (sesame paste)
tamarind paste (seedless)
tomato paste/concentrate
vegetable broth powder

# AMERICAS

# AMERICAS

### Decked Out Skater Boy
### Honolulu, Hawai'i, USA. 12/1987

The elevator chimes gently and the doors open on the third floor of the Ala Moana Shopping Center. I step out. I'm 13 years old and I've been waiting an eternity for this moment. It's been a long six months! Up ahead, I can already see T&C Surf & Skate Designs. The rubber soles of my Vision Street Wear shoes slap and squeak on the polished floor tiles as I anxiously approach the shop.

I check the rolls on my hot pink t-shirt sleeves – they're fine. My superfluous suspenders hang perfectly in half-moon loops at my hips. My bleached blonde bangs need a quick adjustment, and then I'm almost ready to go in. I glance at my turquoise Swatch. Exactly 81 minutes before I have to meet my parents and little brothers back at the high-rise hotel.

I head straight to the wall of skateboard decks. It's immense and overwhelming – it's like the menu at the awesome Japanese grill restaurant last night – I want everything.

Oh god, it's going to be impossible to choose!

### How Do You Say I'm Sorry in Vietnamese?
### Toronto, Canada. 10/1994

After late morning bowls of ramen, we left Trenton, New Jersey in Chinh's '84 Honda Accord.

It took us most of the Cocteau Twins' early discography, a couple This Mortal Coil albums, and several other 4AD cassette tapes to get to Montreal.

We slept on the living room floor of his uncle's tiny ground floor apartment. It was like a temple – golden Buddhist figurines and paintings adorned an entire wall. There was a fountain of water running over dark stones, potted bamboo plants that reached the ceiling, and a shrine with black & white photographs of family members. The room smelled rich of burning incense, familiar from my favorite grocery shops and the homes of various childhood friends.

We drove on after a simple breakfast. By time we had arrived at his cousin's house in the flat, sprawling suburbs of Toronto, we'd listened to every album by The Cure. And we were hungry – the way art school students always are. His cousin informed us that we were obnoxiously early, the kitchen was off-limits as his grandmother and aunt were cooking an entirely vegetarian, epic family dinner; We should go downtown for a while to get out of the way. So we did.

When we returned the house was full of more aunts, uncles, and cousins. And it smelled heavenly! Every counter and table in the kitchen and dining room was covered with abundant platters of stunning vegetable, noodle, and rice dishes. Deep-fried rolls, fresh rolls, steaming buns and dumplings, sensational salads, and sauces filled every gap.

Plates were handed out and I began to heap generous portions of everything onto my plate. There was so much... and it looked SO GOOD! I couldn't wait to try it all!

Soon my plate was a mountain of traditional deliciousness. I was flooded with anxious gratitude – you know, when your thoughts are spinning wildly because you just can't believe how lucky you are.

I sat down and realized it was dead quiet. Was someone about to say a prayer? Then the grandmother spoke in Vietnamese. Everyone burst out in laughter. Except Chinh – whose face was red with embarrassment.

"She said 'Your friend must be very hungry,'" he muttered, and pointed at my ridiculously overloaded plate.

That's when I saw that everyone else's plates had tiny servings of just a few things.

## Lonely Rider
### Boston – San Francisco, USA. 05/1998

Left Los Angeles this morning at dawn. Absolutely glorious to drive the motorcycle up the legendary Pacific Coast Highway; winding my way up the California coast. Watching the wetsuited surfers in the early morning Malibu waves. The adorable seals sunning themselves on the rocks of Big Sur. A picnic on the lawn at Henry Miller's place.

The rain started outside Santa Cruz and soaked me to the city limits of San Francisco. It was so surreal – just when the destination of this odyssey came into view, the clouds cleared and amber light lit up everything.

I cried inside my helmet. I am here!

Hard to believe just three days ago I woke up in a tent in the Mohave desert. Two days before that I was gazing at the Grand Canyon. Heavy snow across the Rocky Mountains. Engine trouble at elevation – until I swapped out the spark plugs in Boulder. Four hundred miles of wind and wheat across plains and prairies of Kansas. St. Louis. Columbus. Philadelphia. New York. Couches. Floors. Borrowed beds. So long ago.

Questioning my sanity every single hour. Laying down to sleep at night, still buzzing and clenching invisible grips, wondering if I really made it. If I'm really still alive or somehow aware beyond death.

I'm addicted to the rhythm of the road but anxious to anchor here for a few delicious days before motoring through more unknown land, unpredictable weather, and a lot more zen all the way back to Boston.

## White Lady & Smoking Mountain
### Amecameca, Mexico. 12/2000

Two more days of acclimatization were behind us. Dad, Adam, and I had hiked six hours from Paso de Cortes to La Joya, the base camp for climbs to the summit of Iztaccíhuatl. Minor headaches and shortness of breath for me, but both of them were really not doing well.

Dad had already set up the tent and started making chili on the camp stove. But as night began to fall, it was clear we needed to get down to a lower altitude again.

We hitched a ride back to the town of Amecameca. Checked into a basic hotel a few blocks from the main square – full of festive lights, ridiculously loud music, and spirited street vendors. The snacks were great and I loved chatting with the locals in Spanish. Definitely good practice before meeting up with our climbing guide and his son the next day. Neither speak English, but Adam's Spanish is stronger than mine. We'd manage.

*"¿Por qué la montaña hace tanto humo, José?"* I asked our guide several hours into our climb the next day. He pointed at the plumes of dark smoke rising from the neighboring peak across the pass and casually replied, *"Está bien. Popocatépetl siempre hace así."*

"He says the mountain always looks like that, Dad. It's fine." Adam nodded in agreement, but I could see he wasn't doing fine. Dad looked worse. He needed to stop every few minutes. It was concerning. I was nervous thinking about the crampons in my pack – it would be my first time trudging up an icy slope at 5000 meters. But the lunar landscape was literally breathtaking.

I decided to just enjoy the volcanic views and keep an eye on them.

We pressed on to the refugio, an aluminum shelter where we hoped to rest before a pre-dawn summit bid. After a couple sleepless hours in the wooden bunks we struggled out into the moonlight and looked at the steep, rocky path ahead.

It was a tough call, but we decided it would be best to descend. Once back to La Joya, José called a friend who drove us two hours in contemplative, crestfallen silence all the way back to Ciudad de México.

The next day, tens of thousands of residents near the twin volcanoes were evacuated when Popocatépetl erupted more fiercely than it had in over 1200 years.

# Salade à la Montréal
## arugula, pears, walnuts & lemon balsamic dressing

serves 2 / time 20 min

**arugula pear walnut salad:**
>    2 cups (70 g) fresh arugula (rocket) greens
>    1 medium (100 g) pear thinly sliced
>    1/4 cup (30 g) walnuts
>    1 tsp olive oil
>    1/4 tsp black pepper ground
>    1/4 tsp salt
>    1 tsp sugar

1. Rinse and dry **arugula**. Transfer to a large bowl and set aside.
2. Heat **olive oil** in small frying pan on medium heat. Add sliced **pear**. Sprinkle with about 1/8 tsp ground **black pepper** and 1/8 tsp **salt**. Sear until soft and browned, about 2–3 min each side, stirring regularly. Transfer slices to a plate to cool.
3. Add **walnuts** to pan. Lightly roast on medium heat, stirring regularly, about 2–3 min.
4. Add 1/8 tsp ground **black pepper** and 1/8 tsp **salt**, followed by **sugar**. Mix well until sugar melts and coats walnuts, about 30–60 sec. Remove from heat immediately if it starts to burn or smoke. Transfer caramelized walnuts to another plate to cool.

**lemon balsamic dressing:**
>    1 Tbs olive oil
>    1 Tbs lemon juice
>    2 tsp balsamic vinegar
>    1 tsp sugar or agave syrup
>    1–2 Tbs water
>    1/4 tsp black pepper ground
>    1/4 tsp salt

1. Whisk all **dressing ingredients** in a bowl or cup. Adjust to taste.
2. Add dressing to arugula greens and toss several times to mix.
3. Arrange arugula with dressing on plates. Top with seared pears and caramelized walnuts and serve.

**Variations:**
**Raspberry**: Substitute 1 tsp raspberry jam for agave syrup. **Apples**: Granny Smith or other crisp apples work in place of pears. **Nuts**: Lightly roasted sunflower seeds, pecans, or other nuts can be used in place of walnuts.

# Lower East Side Salad
## avocado & tomatoes on quinoa & carrot ginger dressing

serves 3 to 4 / time 25 min

**1 cup (180 g) quinoa**
**1 3/4 cups (420 ml) water**
**1/4 tsp salt**
**1 small (140 g) avocado** chopped
**6–8 medium (100 g) cherry tomatoes** chopped
**small handful fresh coriander** or **parsley** chopped, for garnish

**carrot ginger dressing:**
**1 small (70 g) carrot** peeled, chopped
**1/2 in (1 cm) fresh ginger** chopped
**1/4 cup (30 g) sunflower seeds**
**2 Tbs (15 g) sesame seeds**
**2 Tbs olive oil**
**2 Tbs lemon juice**
**1 Tbs agave syrup**
**1 Tbs soy sauce**
**1/4 cup (60 ml) water** more as needed
**1/4 tsp salt**

1. Heat a small pan on medium heat. Lightly roast **sunflower seeds**, stirring often, about 2–3 min. Add sesame seeds and continue to roast for another 1–2 min. Remove from heat.
2. Rinse and drain **quinoa** thoroughly.
3. Bring 1 3/4 cups (420 ml) **water** to boil in a small pot. Add **quinoa** and 1/4 tsp **salt**. Cover and steam until liquid is absorbed, about 20 min. Remove from heat. Stir gently with a fork. Cover and let sit for 10 min.
4. Blend all dressing ingredients (including roasted seeds and nuts) in a blender or food processor until smooth, adding slightly more water if needed. Adjust salt to taste.
5. Arrange steamed quinoa on plates, followed by chopped **avocado** and **tomatoes**.
6. Pour on dressing. Garnish with chopped, fresh **coriander** or **parsley**.

# Jersey Summer Salad
## spinach, tomatoes, mushrooms, walnuts & raspberry vinaigrette

serves 2 to 3 / time 15 min

**3 cups (5 oz / 140 g) fresh spinach** chopped
**1 large (100 g) tomato** chopped
**2–3 medium (80 g) mushrooms** sliced
**1/4 cup (30 g) walnuts**

**raspberry balsamic vinaigrette:**
**2 Tbs olive oil**
**2 Tbs balsamic vinegar**
**2 Tbs water**
**1 Tbs raspberry jam** or **small handful fresh raspberries**
**1–2 tsp agave syrup** *optional*
**1/4 tsp black pepper** ground
**1/4 tsp sea salt**

1. Rinse and chop **spinach**. Divide between two or three bowls or plates.
2. Top spinach with chopped **tomato**, sliced **mushrooms**, and **walnuts**.
3. Add **raspberry jam** to a bowl. If using fresh **berries**, mash them first with a fork.
   Add remaining **vinaigrette ingredients** to the bowl and whisk until smooth. Adjust **salt** to taste.
4. Pour dressing over each salad and serve.

**Variations:**
**Strawberries**: Use strawberry jam instead, or add a handful of sliced fresh strawberries to the salad.

# Dad's Pancakes
## American breakfast classic

serves 2 to 3 / time 30 min +

**1 2/3 cups (200 g) flour** (all-purpose / type 550)
**1 Tbs chickpea flour**
**1 Tbs flax seeds** ground
or **1 Tbs corn starch**
**1 1/2 tsp baking powder**
**1/4 tsp cinnamon** ground
**3 Tbs sugar**
**1/4 tsp sea salt**

**1 2/3 cups (400 ml) soy milk** more as needed
**1 Tbs lemon juice**
**1 tsp rice vinegar**
**2 tsp vegetable oil** more as needed

**fresh fruit** (e.g. sliced banana, pineapple, mango, or berries)
**margarine**
**powdered sugar**, **syrup**, or **fruit jam**

1. Mix **flour**, **chickpea flour**, ground **flax seeds** (or **corn starch**), **baking powder**, ground **cinnamon, sugar**, and **salt** in a large mixing bowl.

2. Gently stir **soy milk**, **lemon juice**, **rice vinegar**, and **oil** in a large measuring cup and then add to dry ingredients. Whisk just until batter is mostly smooth, adding slightly more soy milk if needed. Do not over mix the batter. Some small clumps are okay. Cover and let batter sit for 20–30 min.

3. Heat a large non-stick frying pan or a well-seasoned cast iron pan on medium to medium high heat. When a drop of water sizzles and dances immediately on the surface, the pan is ready. If not using a non-stick pan, rub a few drops of oil on the surface of the pan with a kitchen towel or paper towel.

4. Stir batter gently a few times and then pour about 1/4 cup (60 ml) of batter onto the hot pan. Repeat for another one or two pancakes.

5. Cook undisturbed until bubbles form all over surface of pancakes, and underside turns golden brown, about 2–4 min. Pry up edges gently with a spatula and flip pancakes. Cook on other side until golden brown, another 1–2 min. Increase heat slightly if bubbles aren't forming or pancakes aren't browning.

6. Transfer cooked pancakes to a plate and cover to keep warm. Continue for remaining pancakes. Keep in mind, the first few pancakes are often difficult as the temperature of the pan stabilizes. Also note that American-style pancakes are typically not really fried, so go easy on the oil in the pan.

7. Serve pancakes with **fresh fruit**, **margarine**, **powdered sugar**, **syrup**, and/or **jam**.

## Variations:
**Extras**: Add chopped strawberries, raspberries, blueberries, sliced bananas, dates, chocolate chips, walnuts or hazelnuts into the batter just after pouring a pancake.

# Waffles
## American breakfast classic

serves 3 to 4 / time 30 min +

1 2/3 cups (200 g) **flour** (all-purpose / type 550)
**2 Tbs chickpea flour**
**2 Tbs rice flour**
**3 Tbs sugar**
**1 1/2 tsp baking powder**
**1/4 tsp cinnamon** ground
**1/4 tsp salt**
**1/4 tsp kala namak** (black salt) *optional*

**1 1/2 cups (360 ml) soy milk**
**1/2 cup (120 ml)** water more as needed
**2 tsp rice vinegar**
**2 Tbs vegetable oil** more as needed

**fresh fruit** (e.g. sliced banana, pineapple, mango, or berries)
**margarine**
**powdered sugar**, **syrup**, or **fruit jam**

1. Mix **flour**, **chickpea flour**, **rice flour**, **sugar**, **baking powder**, ground **cinnamon**, **salt**, and **kala namak** (if using) in a large mixing bowl.
2. Add **soy milk**, **water**, **rice vinegar**, and 1 Tbs **oil** to dry ingredients. Whisk just until batter is mostly smooth and pourable, adding slightly more some water if needed. Do not over mix the batter. Some small clumps are okay. Cover and let batter sit for 20–30 min.
3. Heat waffle iron on medium high heat.
4. Brush some **oil** on both sides of the hot griddle surfaces. Do this before pouring batter each time.
5. Gently stir batter a few times. Pour enough batter to cover the griddle well and close the iron. Cook until waffles are golden brown, about 3–5 min. Carefully open waffle iron, peel up an edge and remove waffle. (If waffles stick to the iron or are breaking apart, you may need to whisk a bit more oil to the batter, brush the iron with more oil each time, and/or increase the heat or cooking time. If waffles brown quickly but aren't properly cooked inside and/or tear apart when opening the iron, decrease heat slightly.) Transfer cooked waffles to a plate and cover to keep warm.
6. Continue for remaining waffles until batter is used up.
7. Serve with **fresh fruit**, **margarine**, **powdered sugar**, **syrup**, and/or **jam**.

**Variations:**
**Vanilla**: Add an extra 1 Tbs sugar and 1/4 tsp ground vanilla or 1 tsp vanilla sugar to batter.

# French Toast
## American brunch favorite

serves 2 to 3 / time 30 min

**6–8 slices of bread** (slightly stale is ideal)
**2 Tbs chickpea flour** or **wheat flour** (all-purpose / type 550)
**2 Tbs corn starch** or **2 Tbs flax seeds** ground
**1 Tbs sugar**
**1/2 tsp baking powder**
**1/2 tsp cinnamon**
**1/8 tsp nutmeg**
**1/8 tsp turmeric** ground
**1/4 tsp sea salt**
**1/4 tsp kala namak** *optional*
**1 cup (240 ml) soy milk**
**1 Tbs vegetable oil** more as needed

**toppings:**
  **fresh fruit** (e.g. sliced banana, pineapple, mango, or berries)
  **margarine**
  **powdered sugar**, **syrup**, or **fruit jam**

1. Combine **chickpea flour** (or **flour**), **corn starch** (or ground **flax seeds**), **sugar**, **baking powder**, ground **cinnamon**, **nutmeg**, **turmeric**, **salt,** and **kala namak** (if using) in a large bowl.
2. Whisk in **soy milk** and **oil**. Mix until mostly smooth, but don't overdo it. Let sit 10 min.
3. Heat a large non-stick frying pan on medium to medium high heat. When a drop of water sizzles and dances on the surface, the pan is hot enough. (If not using a non-stick frying pan, rub a few drops of oil over the surface with a paper towel before frying each slice.)
4. Dip a slice of **bread** in batter on both sides. Let it soak for a few seconds, then transfer it to the hot pan. Repeat for another slice or two. Fry slices on each side for 3–4 minutes until deep golden brown, turning carefully with a spatula. If slices are sticking to the pan, add a few drops of oil or some margarine around the slices before turning. Transfer cooked slices to a plate and cover. Continue for remaining slices.
5. Serve with **fresh fruit**, **margarine**, **powdered sugar**, **syrup**, and/or **jam**.

**Variations:**
**Orange**: Add 2 tsp orange zest to batter. **Vanilla**: Add 1/4 tsp ground vanilla or 1 tsp vanilla sugar to batter.
**Chocolate**: Use chocolate soy milk or add 1 Tbs cocoa powder to batter. Adjust soy milk accordingly.

# Tofu Scramble
## with mixed vegetables

serves 3 to 4 / time 30 min

**14 oz (400 g) firm tofu** crumbled
**2 medium (200 g) potatoes** peeled, chopped
**1 medium (100 g) carrot** peeled, chopped
**1 cup (100 g) broccoli** chopped
**7–8 small (90 g) cherry tomatoes** chopped
**1 small (70 g) onion** chopped

**2 Tbs vegetable oil**
**1/2 tsp cumin** ground
**1/4 tsp black pepper** ground
**1/4 tsp paprika** ground
**3/4 tsp turmeric** ground
**2 sprigs fresh rosemary** and/or **thyme** chopped
**1–2 Tbs margarine** or **water**
**1–2 Tbs tapioca starch** or **chickpea flour** (besan)
**1 Tbs nutritional yeast flakes** *optional*
**3/4 tsp sea salt**
**1/2 tsp kala namak** (black salt) *optional*
**2 tsp lemon juice**
**fresh parsley** or **other herbs** chopped, for garnish

1. Heat **oil** in a large pan on medium heat.
2. Add chopped **onion**. Fry, stirring often, until onion starts to soften, 2–3 min.
3. Add chopped **potatoes** and **carrot,** followed by ground **cumin**, **black pepper**, and **paprika**.
   Fry, stirring regularly, until potatoes begin to soften, 5–7 min.
4. Stir in crumbled **tofu**, ground **turmeric**, and **rosemary** and/or **thyme**. Fry 2–3 min, stirring regularly.
5. Add chopped **broccoli** and **tomato**. Cook, partially covered, stirring regularly, until broccoli begins to soften and tomatoes fall apart, 3–5 min.
6. Stir in 1–2 Tbs **margarine** (or **water**). Mix in **tapioca starch** (or **chickpea flour**), **nutritional yeast**, and **salt**. Continue to cook, stirring, until liquid is gone and potatoes are soft, 3–5 min.
7. Add **kala namak** (if using) and **lemon juice**. Mix well. Turn off heat. Cover and let sit 5 min.
8. Garnish with fresh **parsley** (or **other herbs**) and serve.

**Variations:**
**More vegetables**: Add chopped mushrooms and/or half a red, green, or yellow pepper along with broccoli. Adjust spices and salt as needed. **Sweet potatoes**: Substitute for regular potatoes. **Vedic Indian**: Replace onion with 1 tsp black mustard seeds, 1/2 tsp fenugreek seeds, several curry leaves, and 1/4 tsp asafoetida (hing), followed almost immediately by chopped potatoes, carrots, and other spices.

# Omelette
## made with blended tofu & chickpea flour

makes 2 to 3 / time 45 min +

**7 oz (200 g) tofu**
**2/3 cup (80 g) chickpea flour** (besan)
**3 Tbs (25 g) tapioca starch**
**1 Tbs nutritional yeast** *optional*
**1/2 tsp baking powder**
**3/4 tsp salt**
**1/2 tsp kala namak** (black salt)
**1/2 tsp turmeric** ground
**1/8 tsp asafoetida** (hing)
**1 1/4 cup (300 ml) water**
**1 Tbs olive oil**
**1 Tbs lemon juice**
**1 tsp rice vinegar**

**3–4 tsp vegetable oil**
**1 Tbs margarine** *optional*

**extras:**
**2 medium (150 g) tomatoes** chopped
**3 large (100 g) mushrooms** sliced
**handful fresh spinach** or **broccoli** chopped
**2/3 cup (2 oz / 50 g) vegan cheese** sliced or grated
**fresh parsley** or **coriander** chopped, for garnish

1. Combine **all ingredients** (except vegetable oil, margarine, and any extras) in a blender. Blend until smooth, about 30–45 seconds on high.

2. Transfer to a mixing bowl or large measuring cup. Cover. Let sit 20–30 min.

3. Heat a small or medium non-stick frying pan on medium heat.

4. Add about 1 tsp **vegetable oil** and tilt to coat the pan.

5. Pour about 2/3 cup batter in the pan. Tilt and swirl pan gently to spread evenly.

6. Add chopped extras as desired. (Don't go crazy or you'll end up with a super sloppy stir-fry.)

7. Cover pan when bubbles appear, after about 20–30 sec. Cook until surface is mostly firm, about 2–3 min.

8. Carefully fold over in half, cover partially, and continue to cook on each side until lightly browned and inside is cooked, another 1–2 min. For the final minute of cooking, add 1 tsp margarine (if desired) to both sides and sprinkle a few drops of water into the pan. Replace cover immediately, and steam to soften the crispiness. (If they're getting very brown or crispy, but not cooking inside, reduce heat slightly.)

9. Carefully transfer to a plate. Garnish, and serve immediately. Continue for remaining omelettes.

# Spaghetti & Vegan Meatballs
## with red sauce

serves 2 to 3 / time 40 min

### vegan meatballs:

1 small (50 g) **carrot** peeled, grated
1 small (50 g) **beet** peeled, grated
1 small (50 g) **red onion** chopped
4 oz (120 g) **firm tofu** crumbled
2 Tbs **chickpea flour** more as needed
1/4 cup (30 g) **sunflower seeds** or **walnuts** ground
1 Tbs **flax seeds** ground or **1 Tbs corn starch**
2 Tbs **nutritional yeast flakes**

1 tsp **Herbes de Provence** or **dried thyme**
1/2 tsp **black pepper** ground
1 tsp **coriander** ground
1/2 tsp **sea salt**
1 Tbs **soy sauce**
1 Tbs **lemon juice**
1 tsp **sesame oil**
**vegetable oil** for frying

1. Combine all **meatball ingredients** (except vegetable oil) in a mixing bowl thoroughly. Add slightly more **chickpea flour** if needed so batter sticks together. Wet hands and form walnut-shaped balls.
2. Heat about 1 in (3 cm) of **oil** on medium high heat in small pot. Oil is ready when a bit of batter sizzles and rises to the surface immediately.
3. Fry 5–8 meatballs at a time in hot oil, turning frequently, until dark brown, but not burnt, 4–6 min.
4. Drain and transfer fried meatballs with a slotted spoon to a plate as they finish. Repeat for all meatballs. These will be simmered in red sauce for the last few minutes of cooking.

### spaghetti & red sauce:

11 oz (300 g) **spaghetti**
4–5 medium (14 oz / 400 g) **tomatoes** chopped
1 1/2 cups (360 ml) **water**
1 small (50 g) **red onion** chopped
2 cloves **garlic** finely chopped
2–3 Tbs **olive oil**
1/2 tsp **black pepper** ground

2 Tbs **tomato paste**
2 tsp **balsamic vinegar**
2 sprigs **rosemary** or **oregano** chopped
2 **bay leaves**
1 tsp **sugar**
3/4 tsp **sea salt**
**small handful fresh basil** chopped, for garnish

1. Bring a large pot of water to a rapid boil and cook **spaghetti** according to instructions, 9–12 min. Drain noodles and toss with about 1 Tbs **olive oil**. Cover and set aside until red sauce is ready.
2. Purée chopped **tomatoes** with 1 1/2 cups (360 ml) **water** in a blender or food processor. Set aside.
3. Heat 1–2 Tbs **olive oil** in a medium pot on medium heat. Add chopped **onion** and **garlic**. Fry, stirring often, until onions are browned, 2–3 min. Stir in ground **black pepper**.
4. Stir in blended **tomatoes**, **tomato paste**, **vinegar**, **rosemary** or **oregano**, **bay leaves**, **sugar**, and **salt**. Bring to boil, reduce to low heat and simmer, stirring often, until sauce turns dark red, 12–15 min.
5. Carefully transfer fried meatballs to simmering sauce. Stir gently to cover meatballs with sauce. Continue to simmer on low, stirring occasionally, 3–5 min. Turn off heat.
6. Arrange cooked spaghetti on plates. Top with sauce and meatballs. Garnish with **fresh basil** and serve.

# Ithaca Mac & Cheese
## baked casserole

serves 4 / time 60 min

**cheese sauce:**

**1/2 cup (60 g) cashews**
**7 oz (200 g) firm tofu** crumbled
**1 cup (240 ml) soy milk**
**1 cup (240 ml) water** more as needed
**1/2 cup (30 g) nutritional yeast flakes**
**2 Tbs tapioca starch**
or **chickpea flour** (besan)
**1 Tbs corn starch**
**3 Tbs lemon juice**
**3 Tbs margarine** or **olive oil**
**1/4 tsp black pepper** ground
**1/4 tsp paprika** ground
**1/4 tsp nutmeg** ground
**1/2 tsp turmeric** ground
**1 1/4 tsp sea salt** more as needed

**10 oz (300 g) macaroni** (elbow pasta) or **shells**

**5–6 medium (80 g) cherry tomatoes** sliced in half
**2 Tbs olive oil**
**1–2 Tbs bread crumbs**

1. Soak **cashews** in hot water for 30 min. Drain and discard water.
2. Cook **macaroni** or **shells** according to package instructions. Drain, return to pot. Toss with 1 Tbs **olive oil**. Cover and set aside.
3. In a blender or food processor, blend soaked cashews, crumbled **tofu, soy milk, water, nutritional yeast flakes, tapioca starch** (or **chickpea flour**), **corn starch**, and **lemon juice** until smooth.
4. Preheat oven to 375°F / 190°C / gas level 5.
5. Heat 3 Tbs **margarine** (or **olive oil**) in a large pot on medium heat.
6. Add ground **black pepper**, **paprika**, **nutmeg**, and any Variations ingredients (see below). Stir well.
7. Pour in blended cashews and tofu. Bring to simmer while stirring. As sauce begins to thicken, stir in **turmeric** and **salt**. Reduce heat to low.
8. Simmer on low for 5–7 min, stirring often. Gradually whisk in more **water** if sauce is very thick. If too thin, continue to simmer until thickened, but still pourable. Add cooked pasta to sauce and mix well.
9. Adjust **salt** to taste, especially if using Variations with more vegetables.
10. Grease a medium large glass or ceramic casserole dish with about 1 Tbs **olive oil**.
11. Pour in pasta with sauce. Spread flat with a spatula. Top with sliced **tomatoes** and **bread crumbs**.
12. Bake until bubbly, golden brown and crispy on top and edges, 30–45 min. Let sit 10 min before serving.

**Variations:**
**Indian fusion:** Add 1 tsp Garam Masala (or 1/2 tsp each ground coriander and cumin) and 1/4 tsp asafoetida (hing).
**Chinese fusion:** Add chopped spring onions, garlic, tomatoes, peppers, pineapple, and 1 Tbs soy sauce.
**Tomato:** Add 8–10 chopped cherry tomatoes and 2 Tbs tomato paste. **Meaty:** Add chopped seitan or smoked tofu.
**Vegetables:** Stir in a handful of peas, chopped broccoli, mushrooms, and/or bell pepper before baking.

# Black Bean Burgers
## with grated carrots & beets

makes 4 / time 45 min +

**1/2 cup (85 g) black beans** (dried)
or **1 cup (7 oz / 200 g) black beans** (cooked)
**2/3 cup (50 g) oats**
**1 medium (60 g) carrot** peeled, grated
**1 small (60 g) beet** peeled, grated
**1 small (70 g) onion** finely chopped
**2 cloves garlic** finely chopped
**1/3 cup (40 g) chickpea flour** (besan)
**1/2 cup (60 g) walnuts** or **sunflower seeds** ground
**2 Tbs flax seeds** ground
**1 Tbs tapioca starch** or **corn starch**
**1 tsp cumin** ground
**1 tsp coriander** ground
**1 tsp smoked paprika** ground
**1 tsp dried thyme**
**1/2 tsp black pepper** ground
**2 Tbs tomato paste**
**1 Tbs lemon juice**
**3/4 tsp sea salt**
**2 Tbs olive oil** more as needed

**4 hamburger buns** or **8 slices fresh bread**
**lettuce leaves** and/or **alfalfa sprouts**
**1 large (140 g) tomato** sliced
**pickle slices**
**tomato ketchup** and/or **mustard**

1. If using dried **black beans**, soak in water overnight. Rinse, drain. Boil in fresh water until soft, 40–60 min.
2. Mash cooked **black beans** in a large mixing bowl. Add **oats**, grated **carrot**, **beet**, **onion**, and **garlic**. Combine and mix well.
3. Add **chickpea flour**, ground **walnuts** (or **sunflower seeds**), **flax seeds**, **tapioca starch** (or **corn starch**), ground **cumin**, **coriander**, **smoked paprika**, **thyme**, **black pepper**, **tomato paste**, **lemon juice**, **salt**, and **1 Tbs olive oil**. Mix well. Cover and chill for 20–30 min.
4. Heat 1 Tbs **olive oil** in a large pan on medium heat.
5. Form 4 burger patties with wet hands. Fry 2 to 4 burgers at a time, 4–6 min on each side, turning carefully.
6. Serve on **buns** (or **bread**) with **lettuce leaves** and/or **sprouts**, sliced **tomato** and **pickle**, and **ketchup** and/or **mustard**.

**Variations:**
**Vedic:** Replace chopped onion and garlic with 1/4 tsp asafoetida (hing). **Softer burgers:** Add 3.5 oz (100 g) crumbled tofu and 1 Tbs corn starch to batter. Adjust salt as needed.

# TLT
## Tempeh Lettuce Tomato sandwich

serves 2 to 3 / time 30 min +

**7 oz (200 g) tempeh**
**1 large (200 g) tomato** sliced
**4–6 large lettuce leaves**
**2–3 sandwich buns** or **4–6 thick bread slices**
**2–3 tsp margarine**

tempeh bacon marinade:
**1 small (70 g) red onion** chopped
**2 cloves garlic** finely chopped
**3/4 in (2 cm) ginger** finely chopped
**2 Tbs vegetable oil**
**2 tsp sesame oil**
**1/2 cup (120 ml) apple juice** or **water**
**2 Tbs lemon juice**
**2 Tbs soy sauce**
**2 Tbs maple syrup** or **agave syrup**
**1 Tbs tomato paste**
**1 tsp Herbes de Provence** or **dried thyme**
**1/2 tsp coriander** ground
**1/2 tsp smoked paprika** ground
**1/2 tsp black pepper** ground
**1/4 tsp sea salt**

1. Add all **marinade ingredients** to a large frying pan and combine well.
2. Cut **tempeh** into slices about 1/2 in (1 cm) thick. Add tempeh slices to pan. Coat both sides with marinade. Let sit and marinate for about 40 min, carefully turning slices and mixing after 20 min.
3. Heat pan with tempeh slices in marinade on medium low heat. Bring to low simmer and cook partially covered until liquid is about half gone, 10–15 min. Flip slices and continue to cook until liquid is gone and tempeh slices are golden brown, crispy, and slightly scorched, another 5–10 min. Remove from heat.
4. Lightly toast the **sandwich buns** or **bread slices** and spread **margarine** on them.
5. Arrange fried tempeh, sliced **tomato**, and **lettuce leaves** on the buns (or bread slices) and serve.

### Variations:
**Tofu Lettuce Tomato**: Substitute firm tofu for tempeh. **Vedic Twist**: Substitute 1/4 tsp asafoetida (hing) for chopped onion and garlic and add 1/4 tsp Garam Masala.

# Three Bean Chili
## with mixed vegetables

serves 4 to 6 / time 120 min +

**1/2 cup (90 g) kidney beans** (dried) or **1 1/2 cups (10 oz / 280 g) cooked kidney beans**
**1/2 cup (90 g) black beans** (dried) or **1 1/2 cups (10 oz / 280 g) cooked black beans**
**1/2 cup (90 g) chickpeas** (dried) or **1 1/2 cups (10 oz / 280 g) cooked chickpeas**

**1 large (120 g) onion** chopped
**2–3 cloves garlic** chopped
**1–2 red** or **green chilies** chopped
**4–5 medium (14 oz / 400 g) tomatoes** chopped
**1 large (180 g) green pepper** chopped
**3–4 large (80 g) mushrooms** chopped
**1 large (140 g) carrot** chopped
**1 cup (8 oz / 220 g) sweet corn kernels**

**2 Tbs olive oil**
**1 Tbs cumin** ground
**2 tsp paprika** ground
**1 tsp black pepper** ground
**2 bay leaves**
**2 Tbs tomato paste**
**1 Tbs balsamic vinegar**
**1 tsp sugar**
**1 1/2 tsp salt** more as needed

**3 cups (720 ml) water** more as needed
**2 sprigs fresh thyme** or **1 tsp dried thyme**

1. If using dried **kidney beans**, **black beans**, and **chickpeas**, rinse and soak them overnight in ample water. Drain soaked beans before cooking. Bring a large pot of water to boil and add beans. Return to boil. Cover and cook until soft, 60–90 min. Drain well and set aside.

2. If using cooked (e.g. canned) **kidney beans**, **black beans**, and **chickpeas**, rinse and drain well.

3. Heat **olive oil** in a large pot on medium heat. Add chopped **onion**, **garlic**, **chilies**, ground **cumin**, **paprika**, **black pepper**, and **bay leaves**. Fry until onions are browned, stirring often, 4–5 min.

4. Add chopped **tomatoes**, **green pepper**, **mushrooms**, **carrot**, **corn**, **tomato paste**, **vinegar**, and **sugar**. Cook while stirring until tomatoes start to fall apart, 4–6 min.

5. Stir in cooked beans and 2 cups (480 ml) **water**. Bring to boil. Reduce heat to low. Simmer for 15–20 min, gradually stirring in another 1 cup (240 ml) **water** or more as needed.

6. Stir in **salt** and **thyme** and continue to simmer on low, stirring in more water if needed, another 10–15 min. Remove from heat. Cover and let sit 15–20 min before serving.

## Variations:

**Vedic**: Omit mushrooms. Replace onion and garlic with 1 tsp black mustard seeds, 2 tsp ground coriander, and 1/4 tsp asafoetida (hing). Substitute 2 Tbs lemon juice for balsamic vinegar. **Pear & Walnut**: Add a sliced pear and 1/2 cup (60 g) walnuts in place of mushrooms. **Soy mince**: Soak 1 cup (65 g) soy mince (TVP - fine granules) in boiling water for 10 min. Drain well. Add before chopped tomatoes and fry until browned before adding other vegetables. Adjust spices, salt, and water as needed.

# Mango Pear Crumble
## with ginger & cinnamon

serves 4 / time 50 min +

**mango pear filling:**
    **1 large (275 g) mango** peeled, chopped
    **2 medium (375 g) pears** chopped
    **3/4 in (2 cm) fresh ginger** finely chopped
    **1/4 cup (55 g) sugar**
    **2 Tbs corn starch**
    **3/4 tsp cinnamon** ground
    **1/4 tsp vanilla** ground or **1 tsp vanilla sugar**
    **1 Tbs lemon juice**

1. Combine chopped **mango**, **pears**, **ginger**, **sugar**, **corn starch**, ground **cinnamon**, **vanilla**, and **lemon juice** in large mixing bowl.
2. Pour filling into a greased medium-sized (e.g. 8–10 in / 20–25 cm) baking dish or cake pan. Set aside while making the crumble crust.

**crumble crust:**
    **3/4 cup (100 g) flour** (all-purpose / type 550)
    **1/2 cup (45 g) oats**
    **1/3 cup (70 g) sugar**
    **1 tsp baking powder**
    **1/2 tsp cinnamon** ground
    **1/8 tsp salt**
    **1/3 cup (80 g) cold margarine**
    **powdered sugar** for garnish

1. Preheat oven to 375°F / 190°C / level 5.
2. Combine **flour**, **oats**, **sugar**, **baking powder**, ground **cinnamon**, and **salt** in a large bowl.
3. Fold in **margarine**. Mix with your hands and form a crumbly dough, adding 1–2 tsp water if the dough is too dry, or 1–2 Tbs flour if it's too wet.
4. Crumble over the filling in large pieces, leaving some holes and gaps. Press the surface down lightly.
5. Transfer to oven and bake until the surface is golden brown and filling is bubbly and thick, 35–45 min. Remove from oven and let cool 15–20 min.
6. Garnish with **powdered sugar** and serve with vegan ice cream, if desired.

**Variations:**
**Other fruit:** Substitute apples for pears, or omit mango and use only pears. **Nuts**: Add 1/4 cup (30 g) chopped walnuts, pecans, cashews, almonds, etc. Increase sugar and add more margarine as needed.

# Roasted Walnut Brownies
## with dark chocolate chips

makes 9 to 12 / time 45 min

**1 1/2 cups (150 g) walnuts**
**2/3 cup (3.5 oz / 100 g) semi-sweet chocolate chips** or **dark chocolate** finely chopped
**1 cup + 1 Tbs (135 g) flour** (all-purpose / type 550)
**1/2 cup (40 g) unsweetened cocoa powder**
**1/8 tsp cinnamon** ground
**1 tsp vanilla extract** or **1 tsp vanilla sugar**
**1 tsp baking powder**
**1/4 tsp sea salt**
**1/2 cup (120 ml) vegetable oil**
**1/2 cup (3.5 oz / 100 g) silken tofu**
**1/3 cup (80 ml) soy milk**, **oat milk** or **almond milk**
**1 cup (225 g) sugar**

1. Preheat oven to 375°F / 190°C / level 5.
2. Lightly roast **walnuts** on a tray in the oven for 3–5 min. Watch them carefully so they don't burn! Remove from oven and let cool about 5 min.
3. Add roasted walnuts to a blender or small food processor. Pulse several times and then grind until fine.
4. Combine **flour**, **cocoa powder**, **cinnamon**, **vanilla**, **baking powder**, and **salt** in a mixing bowl.
5. In a separate bowl, combine **oil**, **silken tofu** (or soy flour / corn starch and water from Variations below), and **soy** (or **oat** / **almond**) **milk**. Add **sugar** and ground **walnuts**. Mix until smooth.
6. Gradually add dry mix into the wet ingredients, stirring continuously. Combine well, but do not overmix.
7. Gently stir in **chocolate chips** or chopped **dark chocolate.**
8. Lightly grease a medium-sized (7 x 10 in / 18 x 25 cm) baking dish or pan.
9. Pour and spoon batter into the baking dish and spread evenly.
10. Transfer to oven and bake until a toothpick comes out mostly clean, 25–35 min. Don't overbake or the brownies will be dry and hard instead of soft and moist. Remove from oven.
11. Let cool at least 30 min before cutting and serving.

**Variations:**
**No Tofu**: Substitute 2 Tbs soy flour or corn starch and 1/4 cup (60 ml) water. **Double Nut**: Add 1/3 cup (40 g) crumbled walnuts (or other nuts) along with chocolate chips.

# Oatmeal Cookies
## with cranberries & walnuts

makes 10 to 15 cookies / time 30 min

**1 cup (95 g) oats** (regular or steel-cut)
**1 1/4 cup (160 g) flour** (all-purpose / type 550)
**1/4 cup (30 g) walnuts, almonds,** or **hazelnuts** ground
**1/3 cup (75 g) sugar**
**1 Tbs flax seeds** ground
**3/4 tsp cinnamon** ground
**1/4 tsp vanilla** ground or **1 tsp vanilla sugar**
**1/2 tsp baking powder**
**1/4 tsp sea salt**
**1/3 cup (85 g) margarine**
**3 Tbs soy milk**
**1/3 cup (90 g) blackstrap molasses** or **agave syrup**
**1/2 cup (60 g) walnuts**
**1/2 cup (60 g) dried cranberries**

1. Preheat oven to 375°F / 190°C / level 5.
2. Combine **oats**, **flour**, **sugar**, ground **nuts**, **flax seeds**, **cinnamon**, **vanilla**, **baking powder**, and **salt** in a large mixing bowl.
3. Add **margarine**, **soy milk**, and **molasses** (or **agave syrup**). Combine well.
4. Add crumbled **walnuts** and **cranberries** (and/or extras, see Variations below).
5. Form 10–15 small balls and place them well spaced on a baking tray lined with baking paper. Gently press them mostly flat. If they don't all fit on one tray, you can do a second batch.
6. Bake for 12–15 minutes until deep golden brown. Remove from the oven. Let cool 15–20 min.

## Variations:
**Other dried fruit**: Substitute raisins, chopped dates or dried apricots for cranberries. **Cocoa Choco**: Add 1–2 Tbs cocoa powder and a handful of chocolate chips. **Cinnamon Icing**: Whisk 3 Tbs powdered sugar, 1/2 tsp ground cinnamon, and 3/4 tsp soy milk in a small bowl. Drizzle over cooled cookies and let sit 20 min.

# Guacamole
## Mexican avocado dip

serves 2 / time 10 min

**1 large (250 g) ripe avocado**
**1 medium (100 g) tomato** chopped
**1 small (60 g) onion** finely chopped *optional*
**1 small jalapeño** finely chopped *optional*
**1 Tbs lime juice** more as needed
**1/4 tsp salt** more as needed
**handful fresh cilantro** chopped

1. Slice **avocado** in half. Remove and save the pit. Scoop out soft green insides into a large bowl.
2. Add **lime juice** and **salt**. Mix and mash to desired texture with a fork.
3. Add chopped **tomato**. Add chopped **onion** and **jalapeño**, if using. (For milder flavor and added crunch, soak chopped onion in cold water for 10 min. Drain well before adding.)
4. Add chopped **cilantro**. Combine well. Adjust **lime juice** and **salt** to taste.
5. Use as a topping for tacos, burritos, wraps, and sandwiches, or serve with tortilla chips or fresh bread. Refrigerate guacamole in a sealed container with the pit to retain color and freshness.


# Salsa Fresca
## Mexican fresh tomato dip

makes about 2 cups / time 15 min +

**2 medium (180 g) tomatoes** chopped
**1/2 small (30 g) red onion** finely chopped
**1 small jalapeño** or **serrano pepper** finely chopped
**2 Tbs lime juice**
**1 tsp olive oil**
**1/4 tsp salt**
**small handful fresh cilantro** chopped *optional*

1. Combine **all ingredients** in a blender or small food processor and pulse several times, or blend mostly smooth if you prefer. Adjust **lime juice** and **salt** to taste.
2. Cover and let sit (or chill) for 30–60 min for more flavor.
3. Use as a sauce for tacos or burritos, or as a dip for tortilla chips or fresh bread.

**The Lotus and the Artichoke**

# ASIA

# ASIA

## The Guest in the Window
### Dàtóng, China. 12/1999

The overnight train from Beijing stopped abruptly so many times, just sitting in the darkness, then moving on again suddenly. I barely slept at all, and arrived to this industrial city utterly exhausted. Checked into an unspectacular business hotel, stashed my backpack in a simple room and made my way out to the bitter cold, smog-choked streets. A man chased me down the sidewalk with a megaphone shouting, singing, inviting me into an empty restaurant. It looked warm inside, so I followed him and was directed to a table at the front windows. After a while of attempting to decipher parts of the menu with a Mandarin phrase book, I looked up and saw the room was now full of guests, all of them looking at me with bright, curious smiles.

Haven't seen any other obvious tourists in a couple days; I've wondered if I'm even in the right city to venture out to the Yangong Buddhist caves and the Hangshen Hanging Monastery. I'll find out tomorrow. Ever since the taxi driver drove to the wrong hotel on the wrong side of the Beijing last week – because I pronounced it totally wrong – I've been feeling unsure about my otherwise trusty travel smarts. But the mishaps have led to some great moments.

Tonight at the hotel restaurant my phrase book, handwritten notes, and eloquently memorized lines – like "I eat vegetables" – only inspired confusion and giggles from the waiters. But then they disappeared into the kitchen and returned with more waiters and a crew of cooks, each of them holding different foods and ingredients. I pointed at the tofu, aubergine, cabbage, carrots, mushrooms, some greens, and a few other vegetables. I turned down a few undesirable items and made various farm animal noises while shaking my head, just to be sure. They scurried back into the kitchen.

Shortly after that four steaming hot dishes and a massive bowl of rice arrived at my table. I dug in while half the restaurant watched. It was absurdly delicious.

## Street Food Time Machine
### Bangkok, Thailand. 01/2017

The others are fast asleep. I slip on my shoes and take the elevator to the ground floor. I'm out the door, around the block, and into the midnight mayhem of Khao San Road. It's even more absurd, electric, and wild than it was the first time I was here seventeen years ago. The magic is still there, but it's definitely nostalgia rather than newness that overwhelms me now.

There's a woman frying noodles, bean sprouts, and tofu at a street cart on the corner. It might be the same place, maybe even the same face who served me Pad Thai on my first night here in 2000. However unlikely, an amusing thought!

I order and pull up a stool. My plate is ready in a minute. I'm going wild with the toppings – crushed peanuts, fresh lime, garlic chives, roasted chili powder! I dig in and the tastes and memories explode.

I'm right here – but also everywhere I've ever eaten this. I'm in Boston at the Chinatown Eatery talking with Han and gazing at the tattered poster of the Damnoen Saduak Floating Market that ignited my earliest fantasies of coming here. I'm in a Philadelphia loft lit by the glow of a red neon sign. I'm in my mother's kitchen, a college dorm room, at my first apartment, and back in my studio in Berlin. I'm in this century and the last.

It's all one timeless plate of fried noodles and crispy tofu cubes.

## Expecting Pirates
## Phnom Penh, Cambodia. 01/2001

It had been several years since backpackers were last kidnapped by the few remaining Khmer Rouge militants still hiding out in the jungles, but most foreign travelers in Cambodia opted for the recently introduced bargain flights or speedboat rides to get from Siem Reap to Phnom Penh. The planes and pilots were assumedly as atrocious as the unpaved roads, which had more puddles and potholes than driving surface. The six hour speedboat ride, which required helmets and roared down the Tonlé Sap river rocking rural villages with the wake of entitlement, didn't appeal to me either. It took a couple days to track down an elusive "slow boat" which supposedly made the trip in anywhere from three to five days.

Using a Khmer phrase book, nods, hand gestures, and stick drawings in the sand I negotiated with the owner of a large wooden vessel docked at the pier several kilometers from the center of town. Eventually, I was fairly confident that I'd arranged passage for myself and five other foreigners I'd met at the Thai border crossing, and with whom I'd spent the last few days touring Angkor Wat and other temple ruins. Siobhan and I climbed on the motorbike taxi behind the teenage driver and he brought us back to Millennium Guesthouse. We summoned the others from their three dollar rooms and hit the market stalls to collect cheap hammocks, mosquito nets, some fresh fruit, and plenty of packaged snacks.

Back at the docks the next evening, one at a time, we crossed a narrow, wobbly plank to board the boat. The captain introduced us to his skeleton crew of three. They untied the boat and started the engine, which rumbled somewhere deep in the belly of our ancient ark. As the sun dipped below the lush, jungle horizon, we gently motored – we hoped – in the direction of Phnom Penh.

Night fell. We passed through a floating village. Hanging lanterns lit tin shacks on wooden stilts. We continued into the dark and the soundtrack of small electric generators and chatter was replaced by the increasingly loud hum of insects as the vegetation thickened around us. The captain shouted to the crew. They promptly cut the engine and fastened our boat to a large post with ropes. Crouched on the deck, the captain then cooked a one-pot wonder on a portable gas stove, using fresh vegetables he chopped on a circular cutting board and murky river water fetched off the side of the boat. He steamed rice and distributed the food to everyone in small bowls. We ate.

After dinner, the men got a bottle of rice wine and began playing cards. The other travelers and I retreated to our cocoons of hammock and mosquito netting. I listened to a few songs with my Sony MiniDisc player and faded into slumber.

A clamor of activity awoke me – shouting, the rattle of an outboard motor, blinding light beams chasing through the air. Our crew appeared agitated. They shouted back and forth and swung their arms at the shadowy figures on the approaching boat. My thoughts raced, I recalled the black clad boys with automatic rifles that halted our pickup on the outback ride to Battambang and took $5 from every passenger before waving us on.

Here we were, miles from civilization and communication, foolish captives on a boat in the pitch dark wetlands of Cambodia. What if the pirates wanted more than money? Would we live to figure out how to get new passports? Would our families ever know what happened to us? Panicking seemed pointless.

There was nowhere to go. We kept still and watched them draw closer amid the shouting.

"Hey, that guy's got quite a belly!" whispered Siobahn. Her sister Orla replied, "And he's holding something." The pirates on the bow raised a lantern. I now saw that the fat one wore a flowing, white nightgown and was at least eight months pregnant. The other was about ten years old and smiling broadly.

The engine noise stopped and the boats thumped together with a splash. Our captain reached out his hand and ruffled the boy's mop of hair. A third figure emerged and secured our boats with ropes before helping the others onto our ship. The family unrolled thick blankets on the deck near us, turned off the lantern and were asleep in a matter of minutes.

We ate breakfast together in the morning. They got back on their boat and motored towards Siem Reap. We continued on to Phnom Pehn and arrived after two slow, sublime days on the river.

## The Girl in the Red Jumper
## Muktinath, Nepal. 05/2001

Just before dawn, I set off in a light snowstorm from Phedi with a small group of others I'd met in the last eleven days of trekking between remote villages on the Annapurna Circuit, this three-week route that encircles a stunning collection of imposing Himalayan peaks and massive mountain ranges.

We'd already traversed nearly a hundred miles on foot – up and down dense green farmland slopes, through lush rhododendron forests, vast canyons and valleys, over treacherous suspension bridges, around sprawling orchards, and along wind-blasted mountain ridges.

We slept in simple accommodations – usually bunks, wooden shacks, or extensions built onto family homes. At times there were no lodges or guesthouse rooms, and the only place to stay was with the family, wrapped in blankets and sleeping bags on the floor for an all-night snorefest.

4000 meters we'd ascended since the trek began. Today – fate and weather willing – we'd reach the highest point of the trek, and walk across the tallest land pass in the world, Thorung La, at 5416 meters. The climb was cruel. A savage slog for hours on continuously ascending snowy trails, with more false summits than ever. At every ridge you'd think the next was the last and you'd almost made it to the top. But after another round of diminishing power and dwindling hope, another ridge – or three – came into view.

There were stretches where I had to stop after every couple steps just to catch my breath and give my desperate lungs a break. After a brief uphill dash, it felt like I'd just run a half-marathon.

When I finally got to the pass, I sat down in the snow under scores of tattered prayer flags flapping in the breeze. I twisted the top off my thermos and sipped the rest of the ginger lemon tea. My lips were tingling. Feeling slowly returned to my numb fingertips.

Pure bliss. This gorgeous, surreal range of immense peaks, icy ledges, and snowy summits – most prominently, Dhaulagiri – piercing eight kilometers up into the heavens – right here! I snapped several photos of the intoxicating view and slipped the camera back in its pouch.

We began the steep descent to the sacred site of Muktinath, place of liberation, and a destination for wandering saints often walking barefoot for months from as far as South India. Over the next two hours an immense lunar valley spread out before us. The moon rose on an almost immaculate indigo backdrop; a single, delicate cloud hung in the cradle of the sky. The endlessly switchbacking trail led to the tiny village of Ranipauwa.

A schoolgirl in a thick, red knit sweater stood on the path. Wisps of her charcoal hair twirled in the wind. She uncrossed her arms and raised one in the direction of a ramshackle inn named after a Rastafarian icon.

"You're finally here. Now come. Eat. Sleep."

## Last Call
## Hpa-An, Myanmar. 02/2017

I fired up the motorbike and drove through the deserted streets of downtown Hpa-An. I'd actually hoped to leave an hour earlier so I could start the two-hour trek up Mount Zwegabin before the sun came up. I planned to dine with the monks and sleep on the floor of their monastery perched on the highest peak in the region. But I'd been up late listening to Elliott Smith on my headphones again, and was off to a late start.

At the edge of town, I twisted the grip and accelerated on the open road. It was fast for unfamiliar territory, but I was quickly immersed in the two-wheeled thrill of speeding past misty Burmese hills, rice fields, and orchards. The wind in my face, my pant legs and shirt sleeves flapping away – I felt unmistakably alive.

Suddenly, a scraggly dog barked and bolted into the road. On instinct, I swerved hard left and barely missed him. He continued barking and chased behind me as I sped on. I was sobered, acutely aware how things would be different if the stray had leapt a moment sooner. Or had there been an oncoming vehicle. It played on a

vicious loop in my mind, always ending differently, often disastrously. I pulled over at a wooden shack and drank an instant coffee with the shop keeper before strapping my helmet back on and continuing.

I turned and drove through a vast field with hundreds of Buddha figures in endless rows on both sides of the road. I parked where the trail up Mount Zwegabin begins. After an hour of steep trail, concrete steps, and dusty switchbacks, I encountered a Spanish guy on his way down. He had grim news.

Two days earlier, a French backpacker ended his life by leaping off the ledge at the monastery. Just yesterday evening they'd retrieved his body far below. Consequently, the mood at the summit, especially among the monks, was very heavy. And foreigners were promptly prohibited from staying overnight.

When I reached the compound, I removed my shoes and ascended the final steps. A golden stupa came into view, its spire rising above the dome. The smells of simmering vegetables and steaming rice drifted from an open kitchen built next to the pagoda. Monkeys quarreled over the contents of an upturned trash bin.

I struck a large, suspended brass bell with a wooden mallet and walked barefoot to the base of the stupa. I sat there in the shade and reflected on the experiences and interactions of the day. I thought of the near miss on the motorbike that morning. I wondered how many lives were irrevocably altered, how many hopes extinguished by a man's desperate resolve a few days earlier, just a few steps away. I wondered what the last hours, minutes, and seconds of his life were like. I sat with the ghost of a fellow traveler who erased himself before we ever met.

After a while of appreciating the view – and my continued existence, I hiked back down in no particular hurry, exchanging words occasionally with the few others on the trail. I got on the bike, drifted through the field of Buddhas again, and savored the eight kilometers back to town.

## Lost Beaches
### Varkala, India. 02/2018

The birds and the horns of the morning have begun. I was up before them, did some yoga on the roof, then walked to the cliffs. I'm looking down at the thin, sandy coast stretching into the distance. I remember this warm light and the deep blue of the sky, the lush greens of Kerala palms, the grays of ragged rocks and chiseled stones – jetties that spill into the water, temples and shrines perched on the ridge. A worn trail runs down to the beach below.

It's hard to be here and not chase the past and every place I've ever been before. The more I see, the more new places remind me of those I've seen. Strangely, revisiting a place a few years – or decades – later often feels less familiar than a totally new place; somewhere I've never been. The Varkala in my mind is so much smaller and calmer. This one stirs memories of Sayulita and Unawatuna. But this is no Koh Samui or Waikiki.

Mornings are far more peaceful than afternoons and in the evenings this young boardwalk mile lights up and the crowds converge. Maybe I'll run back to the guesthouse, get my swimsuit, and swim before breakfast. In another hour the beach will be hot and busy. But I don't feel like rushing.

Perhaps I'll just sit in the shade and watch the turn of the tides. Retreating waves stealing back the sand. There's one lonely surfer out in the swell, seemingly unsure when to ride in to shore.

# Ma Jiang Mian
## Chinese cold sesame noodles

serves 3 to 4 / time 30 min +

**9 oz (250 g) mee noodles** (Asian thin wheat noodles)
**2 tsp sesame oil**

**3 Tbs peanut butter** or **cashew butter**
**1 Tbs sesame paste** (tahini)
**3–4 Tbs soy sauce**
**1 Tbs rice vinegar** or **2 Tbs lemon juice**
**2–3 Tbs agave syrup** or **sugar**
**1/4 tsp salt**
**3–4 Tbs water** as needed
**1 small (70 g) carrot** peeled, grated
**1 cup (50 g) bean sprouts**
**1/4 cup (10 g) spring onion greens** or **scallions** chopped
**1 Tbs sesame seeds** lightly roasted, for garnish

1. Prepare **noodles** according to package instructions. Drain and rinse with cold water. Transfer noodles to a large bowl and toss with **sesame oil**. Set aside while making sauce.

2. In a measuring cup, whisk **peanut** (or **cashew**) **butter**, **sesame paste**, **soy sauce**, **vinegar** (or **lemon juice**), **agave syrup** (or **sugar**), **salt**, and 3–4 Tbs **water** (as needed) until creamy and smooth. Adjust soy sauce, salt, and sweetness to taste.

3. Pour most of the whisked sauce over cooled noodles. Toss several times to coat with sauce. Cover and transfer to fridge. Chill 30 min.

4. Remove from fridge and add half of the grated **carrot**, **bean sprouts**, and chopped **spring onion greens** (or **scallions**) to the cold noodles. Toss several times to combine with sauce.

5. Portion onto plates or in bowls. Top with remaining grated **carrot**, **bean sprouts**, and **spring onion greens** (or **scallions**). Drizzle remaining sauce over everything. Garnish with **sesame seeds**.

6. Serve with other dim sum dishes, such as Wonton (page 71), or as an appetizer.

## Variations:
**Tofu/Seitan**: Add thinly sliced smoked tofu or seitan to cooled noodles before mixing with sauce.
**Spicy**: Add 1–2 tsp hot chili sauce to sauce before mixing. **Spicy Seitan**: In hot oil, fry 7 oz / 200 g sliced seitan, 1–2 chopped red chilies, 1/2 in (1 cm) chopped fresh ginger, and 1/2 tsp each ground black pepper and coriander. Let cool before adding to noodles and mixing with sauce. Adjust soy sauce as needed.

# Wonton
## Chinese vegetable & tofu dumplings

makes 15 to 20 pieces / time 45 min +

**wonton wrappers:**

1 1/4 cups (160 g) flour (all-purpose / type 550)
1 Tbs tapioca starch
1/2 tsp salt

1/3 cup + 1 Tbs (100 ml) water
1 Tbs vegetable oil

1. Combine **flour**, **tapioca starch**, and **salt** in a large bowl.
2. Add **water** and combine well. Knead briefly and then gradually work in the **oil**. Knead well with your hands 3–4 min to form a smooth, even dough, adding slightly more flour or water as needed.
3. Form a large ball, return dough to the bowl. Cover with plastic wrap and let sit 30 min.

**vegetable & tofu filling:**

5 oz (140 g) firm tofu crumbled
1/2 cup (45 g) cabbage finely chopped
1 medium (75 g) carrot finely chopped
3–4 medium (60 g) spring onions finely chopped
2 cloves garlic finely chopped
3/4 in (2 cm) fresh ginger finely chopped

1 Tbs vegetable oil more as needed for frying
1/2 tsp coriander ground
1/2 tsp black pepper ground
1/2 tsp salt
2 Tbs soy sauce
1 tsp rice vinegar

1. Heat **oil** in a medium frying pan on medium high heat. Add chopped **spring onions**, **garlic**, **ginger**, ground **coriander**, and **black pepper**. Fry while stirring until browned, 2–3 min.
2. Add crumbled **tofu**, chopped **cabbage**, and **carrots**. Stir fry until vegetables are mostly soft, 5–8 min.
3. Stir in **salt**, **soy sauce**, and **rice vinegar**. Fry another 1–2 min, then remove from heat. Let it cool.
4. Pull off a piece of wrapper dough, knead briefly, and roll it out very flat (1–2 mm) on a floured surface. Cut into squares about 4 x 4 in (10 x 10 cm). Repeat to use all dough, making 15 to 20 wrappers.
5. Place about 2–3 tsp cooked filling in the middle of each cut wrapper. Fold opposite corners over filling, press lightly and seal with a drop of water. Fold over other corners and seal again with a drop of water.
6. **Steam-fried**: Heat 1–2 Tbs oil in a wok on medium high heat. Fry wontons until scorched on all sides, 4–6 min. Add 1–2 Tbs water to wok and cover. Steam 2–3 min, stirring a few times, adding water if needed.
   **Steamed**: Arrange wontons in a bamboo steamer basket (or on a lightly greasedplate) inside a pot with about 1 in (3 cm) boiling water. Cover and steam on medium low 7–12 min, in multiple batches if needed.
   **Deep-fried**: Carefully deep fry in small batches in 2 in (5 cm) of hot oil until golden brown, 3–5 min.
7. Serve with soy sauce, hoisin sauce, and/or hot chili sauce.

## Variations:
**Seitan**: Substitute chopped seitan for tofu. **TVP:** Soak 3/4 cup (45 g) soy mince (TVP - fine granules) in boiling water for 10 min. Drain well. Fry with vegetables instead of crumbled tofu. Adjust spices and salt as needed.

# Congee
## savory rice porridge

serves 4 / time 90 min +

**3/4 cup (135 g) jasmine rice** or **short-grain (e.g. sushi) rice**
**6 1/2 cups (~1600 ml) water**
**1/2 tsp salt**

## toppings:
**2–4 Tbs almonds** lightly roasted
**2–4 tsp sesame seeds** lightly roasted
**2–4 Tbs soy sauce** (shoyu or tamari)
**2–4 tsp sesame oil**
**ground red chili pepper** or **hot sauce** *optional*
**fresh herbs** or **spring onions** finely chopped, for garnish

1. Rinse and drain **rice** once. Don't rinse it too thoroughly, or you'll lose much of the starch.
2. Add rice, 6 1/2 cups (~1600 ml) **water** and **salt** to a large pot. Ideally, let soak for 30 min.
3. Bring to a low boil, reduce heat to absolute minimum (on the smallest burner of your stove) and cover pot.
4. Simmer until rice is totally soft, has fallen apart and turned into porridge, stirring only very occasionally to prevent it from sticking to the pot, about 60–90 minutes, depending on desired thickness.
5. Remove from heat, stir a few times. Cover until ready to serve.
6. Garnish with **toppings** and serve.

## Variations:
**Hearty broth**: Simmer several sliced shiitake mushrooms, a large piece of kombu seaweed, and 1 in (3 cm) sliced fresh ginger in 7 cups (~1700 ml) water on low heat for 30 min. Remove solids before adding rice and salt and cooking as above. **Meaty**: Fry some chopped seitan or tofu with chopped fresh ginger, garlic, and spring onions or shallots in hot oil, finishing with a splash of soy sauce and rice vinegar. **Sweet**: Use only 1/4 tsp salt if you prefer sweet toppings, such as sliced fruit, syrup, and jam.

# Horenso Goma-ae
## Japanese chilled sesame spinach

serves 2 / time 20 min +

**6–8 cups (11 oz / 300 g) fresh spinach** chopped
**2 Tbs sesame paste** (tahini) or **peanut / cashew butter**
**1 Tbs soy sauce** (shoyu)
**1 tsp agave syrup** *optional*
**1 tsp sesame oil**
**1–2 Tbs water** more as needed
**2 tsp sesame seeds** roasted, for garnish

1. Steam **spinach** in a covered pot with 2–3 Tbs water until wilted and soft, about 5 min.
2. Drain and press excess water out of cooked spinach. Separate into two portions in small bowls or plates. Transfer to fridge and chill for 30–60 min.
3. In a bowl, whisk **sesame paste** (or **peanut / cashew butter**), **soy sauce**, **agave syrup** (if using), **sesame oil**, and **water** until smooth and creamy, adding slightly more water if needed.
4. Drizzle whisked sauce over chilled spinach, garnish with roasted **sesame seeds**, and serve.

# Misoshiru
## Japanese miso soup with tofu

serves 2 to 3 / time 15 min

**3 cups (720 ml) water** or **vegetable broth**
**3.5 oz (100 g) firm tofu** cut in small cubes
**1/4 cup (15 g) spring onions** thinly sliced
**1 Tbs wakame** (dried seaweed) *optional*
**2 Tbs miso paste** (red or white)

1. Bring 3 cups (720 ml) **water** or **vegetable broth** to a soft boil in a medium pot on low heat.
2. Add **tofu** cubes, thinly sliced **spring onions**, and **wakame** (if using). Simmer for 2–3 min.
3. Stir in **miso paste** and whisk until it dissolves. Remove from heat and cover.
4. Stir a few times gently and then laden into bowls and serve.

# Teriyaki Tempeh
## Japanese stir-fry with vegetables

serves 3 to 4 / time 60 min

**tempeh & marinade:**

**14 oz (400 g) tempeh** cut into small cubes
**1 cup (80 g) spring onions** chopped
**1 in (3 cm) ginger** finely chopped
**3 cloves garlic** finely chopped
**1 red chili** seeded, sliced *optional*

**2/3 cup (180 ml) water**

**1/3 cup (80 ml) soy sauce** (shoyu)
**1/4 cup (60 ml) fresh orange juice**
**1 Tbs orange zest**
**3 Tbs rice vinegar**
**3 Tbs vegetable oil**
**3 Tbs sugar**
**1/2 tsp black pepper** ground

1. Combine chopped **tempeh** cubes and **marinade ingredients** in a large pot or frying pan. Mix well. Marinate (unheated) for 15–20 min. Mix and turn pieces and marinate another 15–20 min.
2. Bring pot (or pan) to low boil. Partially cover and simmer on low heat about 10 min. Stir and turn pieces. Continue to simmer on low, stirring infrequently, until liquid is mostly reduced, another 5–10 min.
3. Increase heat to medium and fry, stirring regularly, until cubes are browned and scorched, 5–10 min. Turn off heat, cover, and set aside.

**stir-fried vegetables:**

**2 cups (150 g) broccoli** chopped in small florets
**1 large (120 g) carrot** peeled, sliced
**1 medium (180 g) red pepper** chopped
**1 Tbs sesame oil**

**3/4 cup (180 ml) water** more as needed
**1 Tbs soy sauce** (shoyu)
**1 Tbs corn starch**
**3–4 tsp sesame seeds** roasted, for garnish

1. Heat **sesame oil** in large pot or wok on medium high heat.
2. Add chopped **broccoli**, **carrots**, and **red pepper**. Stir fry until vegetables start to soften, 4–6 min.
3. Add cooked, marinated tempeh to pot or wok of frying vegetables. Mix well. Fry 2–3 min, stirring regularly.
4. Whisk **water**, **soy sauce**, and **corn starch** in a bowl or measuring cup. Slowly pour mixture into frying vegetables and tempeh cubes, stirring constantly.
5. Simmer on medium heat, stirring constantly, until sauce has thickened, 3–5 min. Remove from heat.
6. Garnish with **sesame seeds**. Serve with short-grain brown rice or sushi rice.

**Variations:**
**No Tempeh:** Substitute chopped seitan or tofu cubes for tempeh.

# General Tso's Chicken
## Chinese-American batter-fried seitan & vegetables

serves 2 to 3 / time 45 min

### batter-fried seitan:

**7 oz (200 g) seitan** drained, chopped in chunks
**1/3 cup (45 g) flour** (all-purpose / type 550)
**2 Tbs rice flour**
**1 Tbs corn starch**

**1/4 tsp baking powder**
**1/2 tsp salt**
**1/3 cup (80 ml) water** more as needed
**vegetable oil** for frying

1. Combine **flour**, **rice flour**, **corn starch**, **baking powder**, and **salt** in a large bowl.
   Mix in **water** (using slightly more if needed) to make a smooth, thick batter. Let sit 20 min.
2. Heat **oil** about 2 in (5 cm) deep in a medium pot on medium high heat. Oil is hot enough when a drop of batter sizzles and surfaces immediately.
3. Add chopped **seitan** to batter and mix to coat the pieces.
4. Carefully slip several pieces of battered seitan into the hot oil. Do not crowd the oil or the temperature will drop and they'll soak up oil instead of frying properly. Fry pieces until deep golden brown, turning regularly with a slotted spoon, 3–5 min. As they finish, drain pieces and transfer to a large plate. Wait 30–40 sec between batches for the oil to heat back up. Continue for all pieces.

### vegetables & sauce:

**2 cups (170 g) broccoli** chopped in small florets
**1 medium (80 g) carrot** peeled, sliced
**2 cloves garlic** finely chopped
**1 in (3 cm) fresh ginger** finely chopped
**1 red chili** seeded, chopped *optional*
**1 Tbs vegetable oil**
**2 tsp sesame seeds** for garnish

**1/4 cup (60 ml) soy sauce**
**1 Tbs hoisin sauce**
**1 Tbs rice vinegar**
**1 Tbs lemon juice**
**2 Tbs corn starch**
**3 Tbs sugar**
**1 1/2 cups (360 ml) water**

1. In a bowl, whisk **soy sauce**, **hoisin sauce**, **rice vinegar**, **lemon juice**, **corn starch**, **sugar**, and **water**.
2. Heat **oil** in large pot or wok on medium heat. Add chopped **garlic, ginger**, and **red chili**.
   Fry, stirring constantly, until richly aromatic, 2–3 min.
3. Add chopped **broccoli** and **carrot.** Fry while stirring until vegetables start to soften, 4–5 min.
4. Stir in whisked sauce. Simmer until sauce thickens, stirring frequently, another 2–5 min.
5. Carefully stir in batter-fried seitan pieces. Remove from heat. Cover until ready to serve.
6. Garnish with **sesame seeds** and serve with jasmine or brown rice.

### Variations:
**Pineapple**: Add 3/4 cup (100 g) chopped fresh pineapple along with broccoli. **Cauliflower**: Use chopped cauliflower in place of seitan. **Vedic Indian**: Substitute an additional 1 Tbs lemon juice for vinegar, and substitute 1 tsp black mustard seeds, 1/2 tsp ground coriander, and 1/4 tsp asafoetida (hing) for chopped onion and garlic.

# Ma Jiang Doufu
## Chinese sesame ginger tofu

serves 2 to 3 / time 30 min

**9 oz (250 g) firm tofu**
**1 small (60 g) red onion** chopped
**2 cloves garlic** finely chopped
**1 in (3 cm) fresh ginger** finely chopped
**1 small red chili** seeded, chopped *optional*

**2 Tbs vegetable oil**
**2 tsp sesame oil**
**1 Tbs sesame paste** (tahini)
**1 Tbs corn starch**
**3 Tbs soy sauce**
**2 Tbs sugar**
**1 Tbs lemon juice** or **2 tsp rice vinegar**
**1 cup (240 ml) water** more as needed
**1 Tbs sesame seeds** lightly roasted, for garnish

1. Cut **tofu** in slabs, wrap in a dish towel. Weigh down with a cutting board 15–20 min to press out excess moisture. Unwrap and cut into triangles or cubes.
2. Heat **vegetable oil** and **sesame oil** in a wok or large pan on medium high heat.
3. Add chopped **onion, garlic, ginger**, and **red chili**. (if using). Fry, stirring constantly, until onion starts to brown, 2–3 min.
4. Add tofu cubes. Fry, flipping and turning pieces regularly, until golden brown, 5–7 min.
5. In a bowl or measuring cup, whisk **sesame paste, corn starch, soy sauce, sugar, lemon juice** (or **rice vinegar**), and **water** until smooth.
6. Gradually stir mixture into frying tofu. Return to simmer, reduce heat to medium low. Continue to cook until sauce thickens, stirring constantly, 3–5 minutes. Stir in more water gradually for thinner sauce.
7. Garnish with **sesame seeds**. Serve with jasmine or brown rice.

**Variations:**
**Indo-Chinese**: Replace onion and garlic with 1 tsp black mustard seeds, 1 tsp ground coriander and 1/2 tsp black pepper. After frying tofu, add 1 chopped small (70 g) tomato and 1 Tbs tomato paste with whisked mixture.
**Nutty**: Substitute 1–2 Tbs peanut or cashew butter for sesame paste (tahini).

# Tom Kha
## Thai coconut soup with tofu & vegetables

serves 2 to 4 / time 30 min

**7 oz (200 g) firm tofu**
**1 medium (100 g) carrot** peeled, sliced
**3 medium (90 g) mushrooms** sliced
**1 cup (90 g) snow peas** or **green beans** chopped
**4–5 small (80 g) cherry tomatoes** chopped
**2 medium (50 g) shallots** finely chopped
**2 cloves garlic** finely chopped
**1 in (3 cm) galangal** or **fresh ginger** thinly sliced
**2 stalks lemongrass** finely chopped
**1 red chili** seeded, sliced *optional*

**1–2 Tbs vegetable oil**
**2 tsp coriander** ground
**1/2 tsp cumin** ground
**3 lime leaves** or **2 tsp lime zest**
**2 Tbs soy sauce** (shoyu)
**2 cups (480 ml) water** or **vegetable stock**
**2 cups (480 ml) coconut milk**
**2 Tbs lime juice**
**1 tsp salt**
**1 tsp sugar**
**handful fresh coriander** chopped, for garnish

1. Cut **tofu** in slabs, wrap in a dish towel. Weight with a cutting board for 15–20 min to remove excess moisture. Unwrap and cut into triangles or cubes.
2. Heat **oil** in a wok or large pot on medium heat. Add chopped **shallots**, **garlic**, **galangal** (or **ginger**), **lemongrass**, **red chili** (if using), ground **coriander**, and **cumin**. Stir fry until richly aromatic, 2–3 min.
3. Add **tofu** cubes. Fry, stirring often, until tofu cubes are golden brown, 4–6 min.
4. Stir in sliced **carrot**, **mushrooms**, chopped **snow peas** or **green beans**, and **tomatoes**. Fry 2–3 min.
5. Gradually stir in **vegetable stock** (or **water**). Bring to low boil. Reduce heat to low. Simmer until vegetables are soft, 4–6 min.
6. Stir in **lime leaves** (or **lime zest**) and **soy sauce**.
7. Slowly stir in **coconut milk**, **lime juice**, **salt**, and **sugar**. Simmer on low for 2–3 min. Remove from heat.
8. Garnish with chopped fresh **coriander**. Serve.

# Pad Thai
## fried rice noodles with tofu, sprouts, peanuts & lime

serves 2 to 3 / time 45 min

**noodles & tofu:**
**7 oz (200 g) flat rice noodles** (3–5 mm)
**7 oz (200 g) firm tofu**
**1/4 tsp salt**
**3–4 Tbs vegetable oil**
**1 small shallot** finely chopped
**2–3 cloves garlic** finely chopped
**2 Tbs pickled radish** (page 146) finely chopped

**sauce:**
**1 tsp tamarind paste** (if using pulp, see below)
**2 Tbs sugar**
**1 Tbs corn starch**
**4 Tbs soy sauce**
**3 Tbs lime juice**
**1/2 cup (120 ml) water**
**1/2 tsp salt**

**garnishes:**
**1/4 cup (30 g) peanuts** lightly roasted, crushed
**1 cup (60 g) bean sprouts**
**handful garlic chives** or **scallions** chopped
**roasted red chili pepper** ground *optional*
**3–6 lime slices**

1. Cover **rice noodles** in a pot with hot (not boiling) water. Stir a few times. Do not boil. Let sit for 20-30 min.
2. Cut **tofu** in cubes. Simmer 10 min in pot of rapidly boiling water with 1/4 tsp **salt**. Drain well. Discard water.
3. Whisk all **sauce ingredients** in a bowl or measuring cup. (If using tamarind pulp instead of paste, soak first in 1 Tbs hot water, strain and use liquid, and discard solids.)
4. Heat **oil** in large pot or wok on medium high heat.
5. Add drained tofu. Stir fry until golden and crispy, about 4–7 min.
6. Stir in finely chopped **garlic, shallot,** and **pickled radish**. Fry, stirring constantly, 1–2 min.
7. Drain noodles. Add to large pot or wok with tofu. Mix well. Cook until noodles soften slightly, 2–3 min.
8. Pour in whisked **sauce ingredients**. Mix well and cook until sauce thickens, 3–4 min, stirring regularly.
9. Stir in 1/2 cup (30 g) **bean sprouts**. Remove from heat. Cover. Let sit 5 min.
10. Distribute on plates. Garnish with crushed **peanuts**, remaining **bean sprouts**, chopped **garlic chives** (or **scallions**), ground **roasted red chili** (if desired), and **lime slices**. Serve.

## Variations:
**Pad Thai Pak:** Fry 1 cup (75 g) chopped broccoli and a sliced carrot along with tofu. Increase sauce ingredients, shallot, and garlic as needed. **Simpler:** Omit tamarind paste or sub 1 Tbs tomato paste. Omit pickled radish or replace with 1 Tbs rice vinegar in sauce. Note: These variations are common, but not traditional.

# Pad Horapa Makua
## Thai stir-fry with eggplant, basil, tofu & cashews

serves 2 to 3 / time 45 min

**1 medium (220 g) eggplant** (aubergine)
**11 oz (300 g) firm tofu** cut in cubes, strips, or triangles
**1/2 tsp salt** more as needed
**3 Tbs vegetable oil**
**2 cloves garlic** finely chopped
**1 cup (80 g) spring onions** chopped
**1 in (3 cm) fresh galangal** or **ginger** finely chopped
**1–2 red chilies** chopped *optional*
**2–3 Tbs soy sauce**
**2–3 Tbs vegan oyster sauce** or **mushroom sauce**
**2 tsp tamarind paste**
**1/3 cup (80 ml) water**
**2 Tbs lime juice**
**2 tsp sugar**
**3/4 cup (15 g) fresh Thai basil** chopped
**1/3 cup (40 g) cashews** lightly roasted

1. Cut **eggplant** (aubergine) in quarters lengthwise and then in 1/2 in (1 cm) thick slices.
   Sprinkle salt on both sides of slices. Let sit for 15 min to sweat. Rinse and dry slices.
   (Skip this step if using less bitter, thinner Asian (Chinese/Japanese) eggplant.)

2. Cut **tofu** in triangles or cubes. Simmer 10 min in a medium pot of rapidly boiling water with 1/2 tsp **salt**.
   Drain well. Discard water. (Alternately, first cut **tofu** in slabs and wrap in a dish towel. Weight with a cutting
   board for 15–20 min to remove excess moisture. Unwrap and cut into triangles or cubes. Adjust salt to taste
   later as needed.)

3. Heat **oil** in a large pot or wok on medium high heat.

4. Add chopped **spring onions**, **galangal** (or **ginger**), **garlic**, and **chilies** (if using) and stir-fry for 2–3 min.

5. Add chopped **eggplant** and **tofu**. Fry, stirring regularly, until golden brown, about 5–8 min.

6. Whisk **soy sauce, oyster** or **mushroom sauce, tamarind paste, water, lime juice**, and **sugar** in a bowl
   or measuring cup.

7. Pour into pot (or wok) with tofu and eggplant. Mix and bring to simmer. Reduce heat to medium.
   Cook, stirring regularly, until thickened, 3–5 min.

8. Stir in most of the chopped **basil** and roasted **cashews**, saving some of each for garnish. Cook, stirring
   a few times, just until basil begins to wilt, 1–2 min. Remove from heat. Cover until ready to serve.

9. Garnish with remaining roasted **cashews** and chopped **basil**. Serve with jasmine rice.

### Variations:
**Pad Kra Pao**: Use holy basil instead of Thai basil. Fry chopped seitan or soaked soy chunks instead of tofu.
**Herbs:** Substitute other fresh herbs such as Italian basil, if that's what you've got.

# Gói Cuôn
## Vietnamese fresh spring rolls with ginger peanut sauce

makes 6 rolls / serves 2 to 3 / time 30 min

**fresh spring rolls:**
  **3.5 oz (100 g) bean threads** (vermicelli)
  **7 oz (200 g) fried tofu** or **smoked tofu** cut in thin strips
  **6 circular rice papers** for spring rolls
  **1 medium (100 g) carrot** peeled, cut in long, thin strips
  **1/2 medium (120 g) cucumber** peeled, cut in long, thin strips
  **handful fresh coriander** chopped
  **handful fresh mint** chopped

1. Soak **bean threads** according to package instructions. (Usually 20–30 min in warm water.) Rinse and drain bean threads thoroughly.
2. Briefly soak a **rice paper sheet** in a large bowl of warm water for 5 sec. Transfer to cutting board.
3. Arrange **carrot, cucumber**, and **tofu** slices on rice paper wrapper. Sprinkle with chopped fresh **coriander** and **mint** leaves. Top with a small handful soaked **bean threads**.
4. Fold left and right edges slightly over ingredients and roll firmly closed from bottom to top, as you would for a burrito or sushi. Pinch and tuck loose ends and sides to seal. Set aside. Continue with next roll.

**ginger peanut sauce:**
  **1/2 in (1 cm) fresh ginger** finely chopped
  **2 Tbs peanut butter** or **roasted peanuts** ground or crushed
  **1 Tbs soy sauce**
  **1 Tbs lime juice** or **1 tsp rice vinegar**
  **1 tsp sugar** or **agave syrup**
  **1/2 tsp hot chili sauce** *optional*
  **1 Tbs water** more as needed

1. Combine all **sauce ingredients** in a bowl. Mix until smooth.
2. Add slightly more **water** for thinner sauce if desired.
3. Garnish with crushed peanuts. Serve with summer rolls.

# Pho
## Vietnamese noodle soup

serves 2 to 3 / time 80 min

**2 stalks (150 g) celery** chopped
**2 medium (250 g) carrots** chopped
**1/2 small (150 g) fennel bulb** chopped
**3 shiitake mushrooms** (fresh or dried) *optional*
**1 cup (80 g) spring onions** chopped, separated into white and green tips
**2–3 medium (60 g) shallots** chopped
**4 cloves garlic** chopped
**1 1/2 in (4 cm) fresh ginger** chopped
**1 red chili** seeded, sliced *optional*
**8 cups (2000 ml) water** more as needed

**1–2 Tbs vegetable oil**
**2 tsp coriander** ground
**2 star anise** (whole) or **1/2 tsp star anise** ground
**6 cloves** (whole) or **1/4 tsp cloves** ground
**1 stick cinnamon** or **1/2 tsp cinnamon** ground
**2 tsp black peppercorns** or **3/4 tsp black pepper** ground
**1 black cardamom pod** (whole)

**5 oz (140 g) flat rice noodles** (3–5 mm)
**7 oz (200 g) fried tofu, smoked tofu** or **seitan** thinly sliced
**3 medium (90 g) mushrooms** sliced
**2 Tbs soy sauce**
**1 tsp rice vinegar**
**1 tsp sugar**
**1 tsp salt**
**small handful fresh coriander** chopped
**1 cup (60 g) bean sprouts**
**2–3 lime slices**

1. Bring 8 cups (2000 ml) **water** to boil in a large pot. Add chopped **celery**, **carrots**, **fennel**, and **shiitake mushrooms** (if using). Simmer gently on low heat about 10 min while preparing remaining broth ingredients.

2. Heat **oil** in small pan on medium heat. Add chopped **spring onion** white ends, **shallots**, **garlic**, **ginger**, and **red chili** (if using), followed by ground **coriander**, **star anise**, **cloves**, **cinnamon**, **black pepper**, and **cardamom**. Fry, stirring constantly, until richly aromatic, 2–3 min. Remove from heat.

3. Add fried spices to pot with simmering vegetables. Simmer on low heat for another 30–45 min, stirring occasionally, gradually adding another 1–2 cups (240–480 ml) water if needed.

4. In another large pot, cover **rice noodles** with hot (not boiling) water and soak for 30 min. Drain and discard soaking water. Return drained noodles to large pot.

5. Strain hot broth into the pot with drained noodles. Discard cooked solids from broth.

6. Add sliced **tofu** (or **seitan**), **mushrooms**, **spring onion** green tips, **soy sauce**, **vinegar**, **sugar**, and **salt**. Simmer gently on low, just until mushrooms and noodles are mostly soft, 3–5 min. Turn off heat.

7. Serve soup in large bowls garnished with, fresh **coriander**, **sprouts**, and **lime slices**.

# Bánh Mì
## Vietnamese seitan sandwich

serves 2 to 3 / time 25 min

**7 oz (200 g) seitan** chopped
**1 small (100 g) cucumber** thinly sliced
**1 small (80 g) carrot** thinly sliced, julienned, or grated
**1–2 Tbs vegetable oil**
**2 cloves garlic** finely chopped
**3/4 in (2 cm) fresh ginger** finely chopped
**3/4 tsp black pepper** ground
**3/4 tsp coriander** ground

**1 Tbs lime juice** or **1 tsp rice vinegar**
**1 Tbs soy sauce**
**2 Tbs water**
**2 tsp sugar**
**1/4 tsp salt**
**1 tsp corn starch**

**1 small fresh baguette** or **2–3 bread rolls**
**vegan mayonnaise** or **margarine**
**handful fresh coriander, mint** and/or **basil** chopped
**2–4 Tbs pickled radish** sliced (Do Chua, page 146) *optional*
**hot chili sauce** (e.g. Sriracha) *optional*

1. Heat **oil** in a medium frying pan on medium high heat. Add chopped **garlic**, **ginger**, ground **black pepper**, and **coriander**. Stir fry until richly aromatic, about 2–3 min.
2. Add chopped **seitan**. Fry, stirring regularly, until browned, about 3–4 min.
3. Whisk **lime juice** (or **rice vinegar**), **soy sauce**, **water**, **sugar**, **salt**, and **corn starch** in a bowl. Add to seitan, mix well. Fry until sauce thickens and seitan is scorched, 3–5 min, stirring often. Remove from heat.
4. Lightly warm and toast **baguette** (or bread rolls) for a few minutes in an oven or toaster oven.
5. Slice bread in half lengthwise, but don't cut all the way through. Fold open. Optionally, pull out some of the soft insides to make room for fillings. Spread each side generously with **mayonnaise** or **margarine**.
6. Arrange fried seitan and top with sliced **cucumber**, **carrot**, **pickled radish** and **hot chili sauce** (if using), followed by chopped fresh **coriander, mint**, and/or **basil**. Fold closed.
7. Slice into sections, if needed, and serve.

## Variations:
**Tofu:** Fry sliced firm or smoked tofu instead of seitan. **Mushrooms:** Substitute 5–6 sliced mushrooms for seitan.
**Vedic:** Replace garlic with 1/2 tsp black mustard seeds and 1/4 tsp asafoetida powder (hing).
**Quick:** Skip the spices, sauce, and frying– just use sliced smoked tofu or store-bought fried tofu.

# Bai Cha
## Cambodian fried rice with tofu, seitan & vegetables

serves 4 / time 45 min +

**2 cups (360 g) short grain jasmine rice**
**3 1/2 cups (850 ml) water**
**3/4 tsp salt**
**5 oz (150 g) smoked tofu** or **firm tofu** cut in small cubes
**3.5 oz (100 g) seitan** chopped
**1 cup (80 g) green beans** and/or **snow peas** chopped
**1 small (70 g) carrot** chopped
**1 cup (80 g) spring onions** chopped, separated into white and green tips
**3 Tbs vegetable oil**
**1 Tbs sesame oil**
**2–4 cloves garlic** finely chopped
**1 in (3 cm) fresh ginger** finely chopped
**1 red chili** seeded, sliced *optional*
**1 tsp coriander** ground
**1 tsp black pepper** ground
**4 Tbs soy sauce**
**3 Tbs water**
**3 Tbs lime juice**
**1 tsp lime zest** *optional*
**2 tsp tamarind paste** (seedless) or **1 Tbs tomato paste**
**2 tsp sugar**
**3/4 tsp salt** (use 1 tsp if using plain tofu)
**4 large lettuce leaves**
**small handful fresh coriander** chopped, for garnish
**3/4 cup (50 g) crispy fried onions** for garnish
**lime slices** for garnish

1. Rinse and drain **rice** thoroughly.
2. Bring 3 1/2 cups (850 ml) **water** to boil in a medium pot. Stir in rice and 3/4 tsp **salt**. Return to boil. Cover and cook on low until liquid is mostly absorbed, 15–20 min. Remove from heat. Stir gently a few times. Cover and let sit 30–60 min. (Traditionally, this dish would be made with about 6 cups leftover, cooked rice.)
3. Heat **vegetable oil** and **sesame oil** in a wok or large pot on medium heat.
4. Add white ends of chopped **spring onions**. (Save green tips for later.) Stir in chopped **garlic**, **ginger**, **red chili** (if using), ground **coriander**, and **black pepper**. Stir fry until richly aromatic, 3–4 min.
5. Add **tofu** cubes, chopped **seitan**, and **carrots**. Stir fry until tofu and seitan are scorched, 4–5 min.
6. Add chopped **green beans** (and/or **snow peas**) and green **spring onion** tips. Stir fry another 2–3 minutes.
7. In a bowl, whisk **soy sauce**, **water**, **lime juice** and **zest**, **tamarind** (or **tomato**) **paste**, **sugar**, and **salt**.
8. Add cooked rice to wok or pot. Mix a few times. Pour in sauce and mix well.
9. Fry, stirring regularly, until liquid is absorbed, vegetables are done, and rice sticks together, 4–5 min.
10. Serve on **lettuce leaves**, garnished with chopped, fresh **coriander**, **fried onions**, and **lime slices**.

# Mirza Ghasemi
## Persian roasted eggplant

serves 2 / time 60 min +

**1 large (350 g) eggplant** (aubergine)
**2 medium (180 g) roma tomatoes** chopped
**2–3 cloves garlic** finely chopped

**2–3 Tbs vegetable oil**
**1/2 tsp black pepper** ground
**1/2 tsp turmeric** ground
**1/2 tsp sugar**
**3/4 tsp salt**
**3–4 Tbs water** more as needed

**fresh parsley** or **mint leaves** chopped, for garnish

1.  Oven method: Preheat oven to 425°F / 220°C / level 7. Poke whole **eggplant** (aubergine) several times with a fork. Rub it with some oil and roast it on the middle rack in oven until charred, shriveled, and soft, 40–60 min. Remove from oven. Let cool 10 min.

    Stove method: Roast **eggplant** whole, directly on a gas burner on a low flame, turning it regularly with tongs until outsides are charred and insides are soft and cooked, 10–15 min. Set aside to cool.

2.  Cut off and discard stems and bottom ends of roasted aubergine. Slice in half lengthwise, scoop out soft, cooked insides into a bowl and discard outer peels. Mash well with a fork.

3.  Heat 2–3 Tbs **oil** in a large frying pan on medium heat. Add chopped **garlic**, and ground **black pepper**. Fry until richly aromatic, stirring constantly, 2–3 min. (If cooking variation below, add crumbled tofu now.)

4.  Stir in chopped **tomatoes**. Cook, until they fall apart, stirring regularly, 7-10 min.

5.  Add mashed, roasted eggplant, ground **turmeric**, **sugar**, and **salt**. Mix well.

6.  Simmer on medium low, partially covered, stirring often, until thickened and oil separates, about 10–15 min, adding **water** gradually as needed. Remove from heat.

7.  Garnish with chopped **parsley** or **mint**. Serve with fresh sangak, lavash, pita or other bread.

### Variations:
**Tofu Egg**: Mirza Ghasemi is traditionally made with eggs. Recreate the taste by adding 3.5 oz (100 g) crumbled tofu after frying garlic. Fry tofu until browned, about 5–7 min, before adding chopped tomatoes. In the final minutes of simmering, stir in 1/4 tsp black salt (kala namak).

# Gajar Masala
## Indian carrot salad with pineapple, dates & cashews

serves 2 / time 20 min

**2 medium (200 g) carrots** peeled, grated
**1 cup (125 g) fresh pineapple** chopped
**4 soft dates** chopped
**1/4 cup (30 g) cashews**

**1 Tbs vegetable oil**
**1/2 tsp black mustard seeds**
**1/2 tsp cumin** ground
**1 Tbs lemon juice**
**1 tsp sugar** or **agave syrup**
**1/4 tsp salt**

1. Lightly roast **cashews** in a small pan on medium high heat, 2–3 min. Transfer to a bowl to cool.

2. Heat **oil** in a small pan on medium heat. Add **mustard seeds**. After they start to pop (20–30 sec), add ground **cumin**. Fry, stirring constantly, until richly aromatic, about 30 sec. Remove from heat.

3. Combine grated **carrots**, chopped **pineapple**, and **dates** in a large bowl. Add roasted cashews and fried spices and oil. Add **lemon juice**, **sugar** or (**agave syrup**), and **salt**. Mix well.

4. Serve immediately or transfer to fridge and chill before serving.

**Variations**:
**Nuts**: Substitute walnuts or almonds. Lightly crush or crumble before roasting. **More masala**: Add 1/2 tsp Garam Masala or 1/4 tsp each of ground coriander, black pepper, and cinnamon to hot oil with other spices. **Fresh herbs**: Add a small handful of fresh chopped mint. **No dates**: Replace with a handful of golden raisins.

# Aloo Raita
## Indian potatoes & cucumbers in yogurt

serves 3 to 4 / time 30 min +

**3–4 medium (350 g) new potatoes** peeled, cut in small cubes
**1 medium (140 g) cucumber** peeled, finely chopped

**2 Tbs vegetable oil**
**1/2 tsp black mustard seeds**
**1 tsp cumin** ground
**1/2 tsp coriander** ground
**pinch asafoetida** (hing) *optional*
**1/2 tsp salt**
**1 cup (240 g) plain soy yogurt** or **coconut yogurt**
**1/8 tsp paprika** ground
**1/8 tsp turmeric** ground

1. Put finely chopped **cucumber** in a bowl and chill in the fridge for 20 min.
2. Heat **oil** in a large frying pan on medium heat. Add **mustard seeds**. After they start to pop (20–30 sec), add ground **cumin**, **coriander**, and **asafoetida** (if using). Fry, stirring constantly, until aromatic, about 30 sec.
3. Add chopped **potatoes**. Cook, partially covered, stirring regularly, until soft inside and crispy but not burnt, 8–12 min. Sprinkle with water occasionally to speed up cooking. Remove from heat.
4. Transfer cooked potatoes to a bowl and let cool. Put them in the fridge and chill 10–20 min.
5. Combine chilled potatoes, cucumbers, **soy** (or **coconut**) **yogurt** and **salt** in a large bowl. Mix gently, but well. Cover and transfer to fridge. Chill 20–30 min before serving.
6. Garnish with ground **paprika** and **turmeric** and serve.

### Variations:
**More Masala**: Add 1/2 tsp Garam Masala and 1/2 tsp amchoor powder to chopped potatoes when frying.
**Golden Raita**: Mix in 1/2 tsp turmeric along with yogurt. **Pink Raita**: Fry a small (120 g) peeled, finely chopped beet along with potatoes. Also add 1 small (70 g) chopped tomato along with cucumber. Adjust salt as needed.

# Poha
## Indian flattened rice with potatoes & peas

serves 2 to 3 / time 20 min

**1 1/2 cups (110 g) poha** (flattened rice flakes)
**1 1/2 cups (350 ml) water**

**3 medium (250 g) potatoes** peeled, chopped
**2 small (100 g) tomatoes** chopped
**1/2 cup (50 g) peas** (fresh or frozen)
**1 small (70 g) onion** chopped
**1/2 in (1 cm) fresh ginger** finely chopped
**1 green chili** seeded, sliced *optional*

**3 Tbs peanuts** or **cashews** lightly roasted
**handful fresh coriander** chopped, for garnish
**2–3 lime slices**

**2 Tbs vegetable oil**
**1 tsp black mustard seeds**

**6–8 curry leaves** *optional*
**1 tsp cumin** ground
**3/4 tsp turmeric** ground
**1 Tbs lime juice**
**1 tsp sugar**
**3/4 tsp sea salt**

1. Cover **poha** rice flakes with **water** in a bowl. Soak 2 min and drain excess water. Set aside for now.

2. Heat **oil** in a large frying pan or wok on medium high heat. Add **mustard seeds**. After they start to pop (20–30 sec), add chopped **onion**, **ginger**, **green chili**, and **curry leaves** (if using), and ground **cumin**. Fry, stirring often, until richly aromatic and onions are browned, about 2–3 min.

3. Add chopped **potatoes**. Continue to cook, stirring often, until potatoes begin to soften, 5–7 min.

4. Stir in **peanuts** (or **cashews**). Continue to cook on medium heat until potatoes are soft, another 3–5 min.

5. Add soaked poha, **peas**, and chopped **tomatoes**, followed by ground **turmeric**, **lime juice**, **sugar**, and **salt**. Mix well, but gently so rice flakes don't get mushy. Cook 2–3 min, stirring regularly. If needed, add 2–3 Tbs water and cover briefly to steam. Remove from heat. Cover and let sit 5 minutes.

6. Garnish with chopped fresh **coriander**. Serve with **lime slices**.

### Variations:
**Vedic**: Replace onion with 1/4 tsp asafoetida (hing) and 1/4 tsp Garam Masala. **Fruity**: Add 2 Tbs golden raisins or chopped dates along with tomatoes. **Coconut**: Add 1–2 Tbs fresh grated coconut along with soaked poha in the last few minutes of cooking.

# Gobi Tikka
## North Indian roasted cauliflower

serves 3 to 4 / time 45 min

**4 cups (400 g) cauliflower** chopped
**1 medium (90 g) tomato** chopped
**1 1/2 in (4 cm) fresh ginger** finely chopped
**2 cloves garlic** finely chopped

**2 tsp tamarind paste** (seedless)
**1 Tbs lemon juice**
**2 tsp sugar**
**1/4 cup (60 ml) water**
**2 Tbs vegetable oil** more as needed
**1/2 tsp turmeric** ground
**1/2 tsp cumin** ground
**1/2 tsp coriander** ground
**1/2 tsp paprika** ground
**1 tsp amchoor (mango) powder**
**1/4 tsp black pepper** ground
**1 tsp salt**
**small handful fresh coriander** chopped, for garnish

1. Preheat oven to 425°F / 220°C / level 7.
2. In a large bowl, whisk **tamarind paste**, **lemon juice**, **sugar**, **water**, and **oil**.
3. Add chopped **cauliflower**, **tomato**, **ginger**, and **garlic**. Toss to mix several times.
4. Add ground **turmeric**, **cumin**, **coriander**, **paprika**, **amchoor powder** (if using), **black pepper**, and **salt**. Mix well to coat all pieces with spices.
5. Generously grease a medium large (8 x 10 in / 20 x 26 cm) baking tray or casserole dish with oil.
6. Pour mixture into the dish and transfer to the oven. Bake 20 min. Turn and mix pieces. Return to oven and bake until cauliflower pieces are roasted, scorched, and crispy on the edges, another 10–20 Min. Remove from oven.
7. Garnish with chopped fresh **coriander**.
8. Serve as an appetizer or with basmati rice, chapati (roti), or naan.

**Variations:**
**Coconut creamy**: Add 1/4 cup (60 ml) coconut milk along with tamarind and lemon juice. **Vedic**: Substitute 1/4 tsp asafoetida (hing) for chopped garlic. **Fruity**: Add 3/4 cup (100 g) chopped fresh pineapple and 3–4 chopped soft dates or 2–3 Tbs golden raisins.

# Pakoras
## Indian vegetable fritters with apple tamarind chutney

makes 15 to 20 pieces / time 60 min

**vegetable pakoras:**

2 cups (3 oz / 85 g) **fresh spinach** chopped
1 medium (100 g) **carrot** peeled, grated
1 medium (90 g) **red onion** chopped
1 cup (115 g) **chickpea flour** (besan)
2 Tbs **rice flour**
1/2 tsp **baking powder**
1 Tbs **lemon juice**
1/3 cup (80) ml **water** more as needed

1/2 tsp **cumin** ground
1 tsp **coriander** ground
1/4 tsp **turmeric** ground
1/2 tsp **ajwain** *optional*
1/4 tsp **asafoetida** (hing) *optional*
1 1/2 tsp **salt**

**vegetable oil** for frying

1. In a large bowl, combine **chickpea flour**, **rice flour**, **baking powder**, ground **cumin**, **coriander**, **turmeric**, **ajwain**, **asafoetida** (if using), and **salt**.
2. Add **lemon juice** and gradually whisk in **water** until smooth.
3. Add chopped **spinach**, **carrot**, and **onion**. Mix well. Add slightly more chickpea flour or water if needed to create a sticky, slightly thick batter.
4. Heat **oil** about 2 in (5 cm) deep in a small pot on medium high heat. Oil is hot enough when small drop of batter sizzles and comes to the surface immediately.
5. Carefully push a spoonful of pakora batter into hot oil. Fry 4 to 6 pieces at a time until deep golden brown, turning occasionally, 3–5 min. Do not crowd the oil. If they turn brown immediately or oil is smoking, reduce heat. If they don't sizzle and darken with 2 min, increase heat. Use a slotted spoon to transfer fried pakoras to a plate lined with paper towels or a dish towel. Continue for all pakoras.

**apple tamarind chutney:**

1 medium (120 g) **apple** finely chopped
1 Tbs **tamarind paste** (seedless)
1 Tbs **lemon juice** or **1 tsp rice vinegar**
1/4 cup (60 ml) **water** more as needed
2 tsp **oil**

1/4 tsp **coriander** ground
1/4 tsp **cumin** ground
1/4 tsp **cinnamon** ground
1/2 cup (115 g) **sugar**
1/4 tsp **salt**

1. Whisk **tamarind paste**, **lemon juice** (or **rice vinegar**), and 1/4 cup (60 ml) **water** in a bowl.
2. Heat **oil** in a small pot on medium heat. Add ground **coriander**, **cumin**, and **cinnamon**.
3. Stir in chopped **apples**, **sugar**, and **salt**. While stirring, gradually pour in tamarind mixture.
4. Bring to simmer, stirring constantly. Reduce to low heat and simmer until thickened, stirring occasionally, 15–20 min, adding water gradually if needed. Remove from heat. Let sit to cool and thicken, 15–30 min.

## Variations:
**Gobi Pakora**: Substitute 2 cups (250 g) lightly steamed cauliflower florets for spinach, carrot, and onion. Adjust water accordingly. **Vedic Masala**: Omit onion and add 1 tsp Garam Masala. **Chili & Coriander**: Add a seeded, sliced green chili and a handful of chopped fresh coriander to batter.

# Masoor Dal
## North Indian red lentils

serves 4 / time 45 min

**3/4 cup (125 g) red lentils** (dried)
**4 cups (1000 ml) water** more as needed
**1 medium (100 g) tomato** chopped
**1 small (60 g) red onion** finely chopped
**1 clove garlic** finely chopped
**3/4 in (2 cm) fresh ginger** finely chopped
**1 small green chili** seeded, sliced *optional*

**2 Tbs vegetable oil**
**1 tsp black mustard seeds**
**2 tsp cumin** ground
**1 tsp coriander** ground
**1/4 tsp asafoetida** (hing)
**1 cinnamon stick** or **1/4 tsp cinnamon** ground
**4–6 curry leaves** or **1 bay leaf**
**3/4 tsp turmeric** ground
**3/4 tsp salt**
**1 Tbs lime juice**
**small handful fresh coriander** or **dried fenugreek leaves** for garnish

1. Rinse and drain **lentils**. Bring 3 cups (720 ml) **water** to boil in a large pot. Add drained lentils. Return to boil, reduce heat to low, cover, and simmer until lentils are very soft, 15–25 min.

2. Heat **oil** in a small pan on medium heat. Add **mustard seeds**. After they start to pop (20–30 sec), add chopped **onion, garlic, ginger, chili** (if using), ground **coriander, cumin, asafoetida, cinnamon**, and **curry leaves** or **bay leaf**. Fry, stirring constantly, until richly aromatic, 2–3 min.

3. Add fried spices along with chopped **tomato, turmeric** and **salt** to pot with cooked lentils. Return to boil. Simmer 5–10 min, gradually stirring in another 1 cup (240 ml) **water** (or coconut milk, see Variations below) or more, as needed.

4. Remove cinnamon stick and bay leaf (if using). Stir in **lime juice**. Adjust **salt** to taste. For an extra smooth dal, transfer to a blender or use an immersion blender and blend to desired consistency.

5. Garnish with chopped **coriander** or **fenugreek leaves**. Serve with basmati rice, naan, or chapati bread.

### Variations:
**Vedic**: Omit onions and garlic, use 1/4 tsp asafoetida (hing), and add 3/4 tsp Garam Masala along with spices.
**Coconut creamy**: Add 1 cup (240 ml) coconut milk instead of water in last steps.

# Chole Bhature
## North Indian chickpeas with fried flatbread

serves 2 to 3 / time 60 min +

### chole (spicy chickpeas):

2 cups (12 oz / 350 g) **cooked chickpeas**
or **1 cup (185 g) dried chickpeas**
**3 medium (300 g) tomatoes** chopped
**1 medium (90 g) red onion** chopped
**1 clove garlic** finely chopped
**1 in (3 cm) fresh ginger** finely chopped

**2–3 Tbs vegetable oil**
**1 tsp cumin** ground
**1 tsp coriander** ground
**1 tsp Garam Masala**
**1 tsp red chili powder** or **paprika** ground

**1 black cardamom** or **2 green cardamom pods**
**1 cinnamon stick**
**2 bay leaves**
**3/4 tsp turmeric** ground
**1 tsp amchoor (mango) powder** *optional*
**1/4 tsp asafoetida** (hing) *optional*
**2 Tbs tomato paste**
**2 tsp sugar**
**1 1/4 tsp salt**
**1 cup (240 ml) water** more as needed
**1 Tbs lemon juice**
**handful fresh coriander** finely chopped

1. If using dried **chickpeas**, soak overnight, drain, and boil in fresh water until soft, 60–90 min.

2. Heat **oil** in a large pot on medium low heat. Add chopped **onion**, **garlic**, **ginger**, **cumin**, **coriander**, **Garam Masala**, **red chili** (or **paprika**), **cardamom**, **cinnamon**, **bay leaves**, **turmeric**, **amchoor**, and **asafoetida** (if using). Fry, stirring regularly, until aromatic and onions are browned, 3–5 min.

3. Blend chopped **tomatoes** with 1 cup (240 ml) **water**. Stir into frying onions and spices.

4. Add **tomato paste**, **sugar**, and **salt**. Bring to low boil. Simmer on medium low heat, stirring often, until sauce darkens and oil begins to separate, 10–15 min.

5. Drain and add cooked **chickpeas**. Continue to simmer and reduce, stirring often, gradually adding more water if needed, another 7–10 min. Remove from heat. Remove whole spices.

6. Stir in **lemon juice** and chopped **fresh coriander**. Cover until ready to serve.

### bhatura (fried flatbread):

**1 1/4 cups (150 g) flour** (all-purpose / type 550)
**1 Tbs fine semolina**
**1 tsp sugar**
**1/4 tsp baking powder**

**1/2 tsp salt**
**1/3 cup (80 ml) water** more as needed
**2 Tbs vegetable oil** more for frying

1. Combine **flour**, **semolina**, **sugar**, **baking powder**, and **salt** in a large bowl. Add 1/3 cup (80 ml) **water** and 1 Tbs **oil**. Knead to form a smooth, not sticky dough, adding slightly more water or flour as needed. Gradually work in another 1 Tbs **oil** and knead smooth, 2–3 min. Cover and let sit 30–60 min.

2. Separate dough into 3 or 4 pieces. Knead each briefly and form a smooth ball. Press flat and roll out into circles about 1/3 in (8 mm) thick on a greased surface.

3. Heat **oil** 1/2 in (1 cm) deep in a medium-sized pan on medium high heat. Oil is hot enough when a small piece of dough sizzles and surfaces immediately.

4. Carefully slip a flattened dough circle into hot oil. After a few seconds, press it down gently with a slotted spoon. Repeatedly spoon hot oil onto the top. It should puff up. Fry until golden brown, 1–2 min each side, turning carefully. Drain and transfer to a plate lined with paper towels. Continue for others.

5. Transfer fried flatbreads to plates. Top or side with cooked spicy **chickpeas**. Garnish and serve.

# Hyderabadi Biryani
## South Indian rice with vegetables & nuts

serves 4 / time 45 min

**1 cup (110 g) peas** or **green beans** chopped
**1 medium (85 g) carrot** chopped
**1 small (70 g) onion** chopped
**2 cloves garlic** finely chopped
**1/2 in (1 cm) ginger** finely chopped
**1 green chili** seeded, sliced *optional*

**1 1/2 cups (270 g) basmati rice**
**1 Tbs coconut oil** or **vegetable oil**
**1 black cardamom** or **2 green cardamom pods**
**2 bay leaves**
**1 cinnamon stick**
**3 cloves**
**2 1/2 cups (600 ml) water**
**3/4 tsp turmeric** ground
**3/4 tsp salt**

**3 Tbs vegetable oil**
**8–10 curry leaves**
**1 tsp cumin** ground
**1 tsp coriander** ground
**1/4 tsp asafoetida** (hing)
**3/4 tsp salt**

**1/3 cup (40 g) cashews**
**1/3 cup (40 g) golden raisins**

**2 Tbs soy yogurt** or **coconut yogurt**
**1 Tbs lemon juice**

**handful fresh coriander** chopped
**handful fresh mint** chopped

1. Rinse **basmati rice** thoroughly. Cover with water and soak 30 min. Drain thoroughly.
2. Heat 1 Tbs **coconut oil** (or **vegetable oil**) in a large pot on medium heat.
3. Add **cardamom, bay leaves, cinnamon,** and **cloves.** Fry, stirring constantly, until aromatic, 30–60 sec.
4. Stir in drained basmati rice, followed by 2 1/2 cups (600 ml) **water, turmeric,** and 3/4 tsp **salt.** Bring to boil, reduce to low heat. Cover and simmer until water is mostly absorbed, 9–12 min. Remove from heat.
5. Heat 3 Tbs **vegetable oil** in another large pot on medium heat.
6. Add chopped **onion, garlic, ginger, green chili** (if using), **curry leaves,** ground **cumin, coriander, asafoetida,** and 3/4 tsp **salt.** Fry, stirring often, until richly aromatic and onion is browned, 3–5 min.
7. Add **peas** (or **green beans**), chopped **carrot, cashews,** and **raisins.** Mix well. Fry, stirring regularly, until vegetables start to soften and brown, 3–4 min.
8. Add cooked rice to pot with vegetables. Add **soy** (or **coconut**) **yogurt** and **lemon juice.** Mix well.
9. Reduce to low heat. Cover and cook undisturbed (without stirring) until rice is soft and liquid is absorbed, 4–6 min. Remove from heat.
10. Gently fold in most of the chopped **fresh coriander** and **mint.** Cover again and let sit 10–20 min.
11. Garnish with more chopped **fresh coriander** and **mint** and serve.

# Dhokla
## Indian savory steamed chickpea cake

serves 3 to 4 / time 40 min

**dhokla batter:**

- **1 1/2 cups (180 g) chickpea flour** (besan)
- **2 Tbs semolina**
- **1/2 tsp turmeric** ground
- **1 Tbs sugar**
- **1 tsp salt**
- **3/4 cup (180 g) coconut yogurt** or **soy yogurt**
- **3/4 cup (180 ml) warm water** more as needed

- **1 Tbs vegetable oil**
- **1 Tbs lemon juice**
- **1 tsp rice vinegar**
- **3/4 in (2 cm) fresh ginger** finely chopped
- **1 green chili** chopped *optional*

- **2 tsp baking powder**

1. Combine **chickpea flour**, **semolina**, ground **turmeric**, **sugar**, and **salt** in a large mixing bowl.

2. In another bowl, whisk **yogurt**, **warm water**, **oil**, **lemon juice**, and **vinegar** until smooth.

3. Add whisked wet mixture to large bowl of dry ingredients along with chopped **ginger**, and **green chili** (if using). Whisk smooth, adding another 1–2 Tbs of **water** if needed.

4. Grease a medium-sized (8 in / 20 cm) round metal cake pan that fits inside a pressure cooker, large pot, or wok with lid. Fill the pot with 1 in (3 cm) water and place a saucer or bowl upside down in the middle so the cake pan will sit securely above the water. Bring water to boil and reduce heat to medium low.

5. Add **baking powder** to batter and whisk briskly in a circular motion to combine and aerate the batter.

6. Pour batter into greased cake pan and place it in the pot of simmering water. Cover pot and steam until the surface is firm and a knife comes out clean, 15–25 min. Remove pan. Cover and let sit while preparing tempering and garnish.

**tempering & garnish:**

- **1 Tbs vegetable oil**
- **1 tsp black mustard seeds**
- **1 green chili** chopped *optional*
- **8–10 curry leaves**
- **3/4 tsp cumin seeds**
- **1/8 tsp asafoetida** (hing)

- **1 tsp sugar**
- **2 tsp lemon juice**
- **1 Tbs water**

- **1 Tbs grated coconut**
- **handful fresh coriander** chopped

1. Heat **oil** in a small pan on medium heat. Add **mustard seeds**, chopped **green chili**, **curry leaves**, **cumin seeds**, and **asafoetida**. Fry until seeds start to pop (20–30 sec), then carefully stir in **sugar**, **lemon juice**, and **water**. Remove from heat.

2. Turn the steamed cake over onto a cutting board. Spread mixture over the top and slice cake into squares.

3. Garnish with grated **coconut** and chopped **fresh coriander**. Serve with Tamarind Chutney (page 107) or Coconut Chutney (page 119) and Sambar (page 118), if desired.

# Masala Dosa
## South Indian crêpe with potato filling

serves 3 to 4 / time 45 min +

### dosa (crêpes):
1 cup (180 g) basmati rice
1/4 cup (40 g) urid dal (hulled black lentils)
1/2 tsp fenugreek seeds

1/3–1/2 cup (80–120 ml) water more as needed
3/4 tsp salt
2–3 Tbs vegetable oil more for frying

1. Soak **rice** in a bowl of water. Soak **urid dal** and **fenugreek seeks** in another bowl of water. Soak 6–8 hrs. Drain and rinse both.

2. Using only as much **water** as needed, blend soaked rice and dal to smooth pastes in a food processor or blender. Combine pastes in a large bowl. Mix well. Cover. Let ferment in a warm place, 12 hrs or overnight.

3. Add **salt** and 1 Tbs oil to fermented batter. (If batter hasn't risen, see below). Whisk until smooth, gradually adding water as needed to make a smooth, easily pourable batter. Cover and let sit 20–30 min.

4. Heat a large frying pan (preferably well-seasoned, cast iron) on medium high heat.

5. Put a few drops of **oil** on the pan and rub it around with a paper towel. Repeat before each dosa. When a drop of water sizzles and dances on the surface immediately, the pan is ready.

6. With a measuring cup or ladle, pour about 1/4–1/3 cup (60–80 ml) batter in the center of the pan. After a few seconds, with a spiralling motion spread the batter outward fairly thin into a circle. Drizzle 1–2 tsp oil around the dosa so it runs under the edges.

7. After bubbles appear on the surface and underside is golden brown, about 2–3 min, carefully lift edges with a thin spatula and flip the dosa. Cook the other side for 1–2 min. Flip the dosa over again, put a lump of cooked potato filling on top, roll it up or fold it over, and transfer to a plate. Continue for all dosas.

8. Serve with Sambar (page 118) and Coconut Chutney (page 119).

### masala potato filling:
4–5 medium (500 g) potatoes
1 small (65 g) onion finely chopped
1/2 in (1 cm) fresh ginger finely chopped
1 green chili seeded, sliced *optional*

2 Tbs vegetable oil

1 tsp black mustard seeds
7–10 curry leaves
1/8 tsp asafoetida (hing) *optional*
3/4 tsp turmeric ground
3/4 tsp salt
1/4 cup (60 ml) water more as needed

1. Cover **potatoes** with water in a medium pot. Bring to boil. Cook potatoes until soft, 20–25 min. Drain. Rinse in running cold water. Remove and discard peels. Mash with a fork in a large bowl.

2. Heat **oil** in a medium-sized pan on medium heat. Add **mustard seeds**. After they start to pop (20–30 sec), add chopped **onion**, **ginger**, **green chili** (if using), **curry leaves**, and **asafoetida** (if using). Fry, stirring often, until richly aromatic and onions are browned, 3–5 min.

3. Add cooked mashed potatoes, ground **turmeric**, and **salt**. Mix well. Cook on medium low heat, gradually stirring in 1/4 cup (60 ml) **water**, more as needed, until smooth, mixing and mashing, 3–5 min. Remove from heat. Cover until ready to make dosas and serve.

### Notes:
If your batter hasn't fermented and risen enough (few bubbles on the surface) and you're in a hurry, whisk in 1/4 tsp baking powder along with salt and oil 20–30 min before frying. Also, it takes practice to get the batter consistency, pan temperature, and motions right. As with all pancakes, the first dosa often doesn't turn out well because the pan isn't evenly hot and/or the batter must be adjusted. Keep trying and above all, have fun!

# Sambar
## South Indian vegetable & lentil stew

serves 4 / time 45 min +

**1/2 cup (90 g) red** or **yellow lentils** (dry, e.g. masoor or toor dal)
**4 cups (1000 ml) water** more as needed
**2 medium (160 g) potatoes** peeled, chopped
**1 medium (80 g) carrot** peeled, chopped
**1/2 cup (60 g) green beans** or **green peas**
**3 medium (250 g) tomatoes** chopped
**1 medium (80 g) red onion** chopped
**3/4 in (2 cm) fresh ginger** finely chopped

**2 Tbs vegetable oil**
**1 tsp black mustard seeds**
**1 tsp cumin** ground
**1 tsp coriander** ground
**1–2 tsp Sambar Masala** or **Garam Masala**
**1/2 tsp red chili powder** or **paprika** ground
**6–8 curry leaves**
**1 bay leaf**
**1/2 tsp turmeric** ground
**2 tsp tamarind paste** (seedless)
**1/4 cup (60 ml) water**
**1 Tbs lime juice** or **lemon juice**
**1 tsp sugar**
**1 tsp salt**
**small handful fresh coriander** chopped

1. Rinse and drain **lentils**. Bring 3 cups (740 ml) **water** to boil in a large pot. Stir in lentils. Cover and cook until lentils are soft, stirring occasionally, 20–30 min.

2. Heat **oil** in large pot on medium heat. Add **mustard seeds**. After they start to pop (20–30 sec), add chopped **onion**, **ginger**, ground **cumin**, **coriander**, **Sambar Masala** (or **Garam Masala**), **red chili powder** (or **paprika**), **curry leaves**, **bay leaf**, and **turmeric**. Fry, stirring constantly, until richly aromatic and onions are soft, 3–5 min.

3. Mix **tamarind paste** with 1/4 cup (60 ml) **water**. Stir into sizzling onion and spices.

4. Add chopped **potatoes**, **carrot**, **green beans** (or **peas**), and **tomatoes** to pan. Mix well, cook partially covered, adding **water** as needed, until tomatoes fall apart, stirring often, 5–7 min.

5. Add cooked lentils to simmering vegetables. Mix well. Simmer on low until vegetables and dal are soft, stirring occasionally, adding water if needed, 10–15 min. Remove from heat.

6. Stir in **lime** (or **lemon**) **juice**, **sugar**, **salt**, and chopped **fresh coriander**.

7. Garnish with more chopped **fresh coriander**. Serve with dosa or basmati rice.

**Variations:**
**Vedic**: Replace onion with 1 small chopped tomato and 1/4 tsp asafoetida (hing).
**Traditional vegetables**: Add or substitute chopped cauliflower, eggplant (aubergine), okra, drumsticks, etc. Adjust salt as needed.

# Coconut Chutney
## South Indian condiment

makes about 1 cup / time 15 min +

**1/3 cup (30 g) fresh coconut** grated
or **1/4 cup (20 g) dry grated coconut + 2 Tbs hot water**
**1/2 in (1 cm) fresh ginger** finely chopped
**1/2 green chili** seeded, sliced *optional*
**small handful fresh coriander** chopped

**1 Tbs vegetable oil**
**1 tsp black mustard seeds**
**1 tsp urid dal** (hulled, split black lentils) *optional*
**1 tsp chana dal** *optional*
**2 tsp lime juice** or **lemon juice** more as needed
**1 tsp sugar**
**1/2 tsp salt** more as needed
**1/2 cup (120 ml) water** more as needed

1.  If using **dry grated coconut**, first mix with 2 Tbs hot water in a small bowl. Let soak 15 min.
2.  Heat **oil** in a small frying pan on medium high heat. Add **mustard seeds**. After they start to pop (20–30 sec) add **urid dal** and **chana dal** (if using). Fry, stirring regularly, 1 min. Remove from heat.
3.  Add grated **coconut**, chopped **ginger**, **green chili** (if using), **coriander**, **lime** (or **lemon**) **juice**, **sugar**, **salt**, and fried mustard seeds and dal to a small food processor. Pulse several times to mix. Adding **water** gradually as needed, blend to a coarse paste, 10–20 sec. Alternately, use a mortar and pestle.
4.  Adjust salt and lime (or lemon) juice to taste. Transfer to a bowl.
5.  Chill 30–60 min in fridge before serving, or serve at room temperature with dosa and sambar, or pakoras.

### Variations:
**Mint**: Substitute chopped fresh mint for coriander. Optionally add 1–2 Tbs plain soy or coconut yogurt. Adjust water and salt as needed.

# Paneer Makhani
## North Indian creamy tomato sauce with tofu paneer

serves 2 to 3 / time 45 min +

**tofu paneer:**
   7 oz (200 g) tofu
   2 Tbs lemon juice
   1 Tbs soy sauce
   2 Tbs nutritional yeast flakes or chickpea flour (besan)
   2 Tbs corn starch
   2–3 Tbs coconut oil or vegetable oil

1. Cut **tofu** in slabs and wrap in a dish towel. Weight with a cutting board for 15–20 min to remove excess moisture. Unwrap and cut into triangles or cubes
2. Combine **lemon juice**, **soy sauce**, **nutritional yeast flakes** (or **chickpea flour**), and **corn starch** in bowl. Add tofu cubes, mix well, coat all pieces.
3. Heat **oil** in a small frying pan on medium high. Fry battered cubes evenly in batches until golden brown, turning regularly, 4–6 min. Remove, drain, set aside.

**tomato cream curry:**

   2/3 cup (80 g) cashews
   2 medium (180 g) tomatoes chopped
   2 1/2 cups (600 ml) water
   1 in (3 cm) fresh ginger finely chopped
   2 cloves garlic finely chopped *optional*
   fresh coriander leaves chopped, for garnish

   2 Tbs vegetable oil
   1 tsp black mustard seeds
   4–6 curry leaves or 2 bay leaves

   1 tsp coriander ground
   1 tsp cumin ground
   1 tsp Garam Masala
   1/4 tsp asafoetida (hing) *optional*
   2 Tbs tomato paste
   1 tsp red chili powder or paprika ground
   3/4 tsp turmeric ground
   1 Tbs lemon juice
   2 tsp sugar
   1 1/4 tsp salt

1. Soak **cashews** in a bowl of boiling hot water for 30 min. Drain and discard water.
2. Blend chopped **tomatoes** with 1 1/4 cups (300 ml) **water** in a blender or food processor until smooth.
3. Heat **oil** in a large pot on medium heat. Add **mustard seeds**. After they start to pop (20–30 sec), add chopped **garlic** (if using), **ginger**, **curry leaves** or **bay leaves**, ground **coriander**, **cumin**, **Garam Masala**, and **asafoetida** (if using). Fry, stirring often, until richly aromatic, 2–3 min.
4. Stir in blended tomatoes. Bring to simmer and reduce to medium low heat. Cook, stirring often, until sauce is reduced and turns dark red, 10–15 min.
5. Blend soaked cashews with 1 1/4 cups (300 ml) **water** until smooth. Stir into simmering tomato sauce.
6. Stir in **tomato paste**, **red chili powder** (or **paprika**), **turmeric**, **lemon juice**, **sugar**, and **salt**. Return to simmer. Cook, stirring often, until sauce thickens and oil begins to separate, 5–8 min.
7. Stir in fried tofu cubes. Continue to simmer on low, stirring occasionally, 4–5 min. Remove from heat.
8. Garnish with chopped **fresh coriander**. Serve with basmati rice, chapati (roti), or naan.

# Palak Paneer
## North Indian spinach with tofu paneer

serves 2 / time 45 min

**tofu paneer:**
>  **7 oz (200 g) tofu**
>  **2 Tbs lemon juice**
>  **1 Tbs soy sauce**
>  **2 Tbs nutritional yeast flakes** or **chickpea flour** (besan)
>  **2 Tbs corn starch**
>  **2–3 Tbs coconut oil** or **vegetable oil**

1. Cut **tofu** in slabs and wrap in a dish towel. Weight with a cutting board for 15–20 min to remove excess moisture. Unwrap and cut into triangles or cubes
2. Combine **lemon juice**, **soy sauce**, **nutritional yeast flakes** (or **chickpea flour**), and **corn starch** in bowl. Add tofu cubes, mix well, coat all pieces.
3. Heat **oil** in a small frying pan on medium high. Fry battered cubes evenly in batches until golden brown, turning regularly, 4–6 min. Remove, drain, set aside.

**palak (spinach) curry:**

>  **4 cups (7 oz / 200 g) spinach** chopped
>  **2 medium (180 g) tomatoes** chopped
>  **1 small (70 g) red onion** chopped *optional*
>  **1 clove garlic** finely chopped *optional*
>  **1/2 in (1 cm) fresh ginger** finely chopped
>  **1 small green chili** seeded, sliced *optional*
>  **fresh coriander leaves** chopped, for garnish
>
>  **1 cup (240 ml) soy milk** or **water**
>  **1 Tbs lemon juice**

>  **1–2 Tbs vegetable oil**
>  **1 tsp black mustard seeds**
>  **4–6 curry leaves**
>  **1 tsp coriander** ground
>  **1 tsp cumin** ground
>  **1/2 tsp Garam Masala**
>  **1/4 tsp turmeric** ground
>  **1/4 tsp asafoetida** (hing) *optional*
>
>  **1 tsp sugar**
>  **3/4 tsp salt**

1. Blend chopped **tomatoes** and **soy milk** (or **water**) in a blender or food processor until smooth.
2. Heat **oil** in a large pot on medium heat. Add **mustard seeds**. After they start to pop (20–30 sec), stir in chopped **onion** and **garlic** (if using), **ginger**, **green chili** (if using), **curry leaves,** ground **coriander, cumin, Garam Masala, turmeric,** and **asafoetida**. Fry, stirring often, until richly aromatic, 2–3 min.
3. Stir in blended tomatoes, **sugar,** and **salt**. Bring to simmer and reduce to low heat. Cook 10–15 min.
4. Add **spinach**. Mix well. Partially cover and simmer until spinach has shrunk and is mostly cooked, 4–6 min.
5. For a smoother curry: Remove from heat, blend briefly with an immersion blender. Alternately, transfer curry to blender and pulse a few times on low, then return to pot.
6. Stir in fried tofu cubes and **lemon juice**. Simmer on low, partially covered, 4–5 min. Remove from heat.
7. Garnish with chopped **fresh coriander**. Serve with basmati rice, chapati (roti), or naan.

**Variations:**
**Aloo Palak:** Fry 2–3 chopped medium potatoes until golden brown and soft. Add to simmering spinach curry instead of fried tofu cubes. **Coconut:** Replace soy milk with coconut milk. **Rich & Creamy:** Blend tomatoes with 2–3 Tbs cashews and 1 Tbs tomato paste. For all variations, adjust water and salt as needed.

# Matar Paneer
## North Indian peas with tofu paneer

serves 2 / time 45 min

**tofu paneer:**
- 7 oz (200 g) tofu
- 2 Tbs lemon juice
- 1 Tbs soy sauce
- 2 Tbs nutritional yeast flakes or chickpea flour (besan)
- 2 Tbs corn starch
- 2–3 Tbs coconut oil or vegetable oil

1. Cut **tofu** in slabs and wrap in a dish towel. Weight with a cutting board for 15–20 min to remove excess moisture. Unwrap and cut into triangles or cubes

2. Combine **lemon juice**, **soy sauce**, **nutritional yeast flakes** (or **chickpea flour**), and **corn starch** in bowl. Add tofu cubes, mix well, coat all pieces.

3. Heat **oil** in a small frying pan on medium high. Fry battered cubes evenly in batches until golden brown, turning regularly, 4–6 min. Remove, drain, set aside.

**matar (peas) curry:**
- 2 cups (8 oz / 220 g) peas
- 2 medium (180 g) tomatoes chopped
- 1 small (70 g) red onion chopped *optional*
- 1 clove garlic finely chopped *optional*
- 3/4 in (2 cm) fresh ginger finely chopped
- 1 small green chili seeded, sliced *optional*
- fresh coriander leaves chopped, for garnish

- 3/4 cup (180 ml) water more as needed
- 1 Tbs lemon juice

- 1–2 Tbs vegetable oil
- 1 tsp black mustard seeds
- 4–6 curry leaves
- 1 tsp coriander ground
- 1/2 tsp cumin ground
- 1/2 tsp Garam Masala
- 1/2 tsp turmeric ground
- 1/4 tsp asafoetida (hing) *optional*
- 1 tsp sugar
- 3/4 tsp salt

1. Blend chopped **tomatoes** with 3/4 cup (180 ml) **water** in a blender or food processor until smooth.

2. Heat **oil** in a large pot on medium heat. Add **mustard seeds**. After they start to pop (20–30 sec), add chopped **onion** and **garlic** (if using), **ginger**, **green chili** (if using), **curry leaves,** ground **coriander**, **cumin, Garam Masala, turmeric**, and **asafoetida**. Fry, stirring often, until richly aromatic, 2–3 min.

3. Stir in blended tomatoes. Bring to simmer and reduce to medium low heat. Cook, stirring often, until sauce is reduced and turns dark red, 10–15 min.

4. Stir in **peas**. Continue to simmer, stirring often, adding water if needed, until peas are tender, 3–5 min.

5. Stir in fried tofu cubes, **lemon juice**, **sugar**, and **salt**. Simmer on low, stirring occasionally, 4–5 min.

6. Garnish with chopped **fresh coriander**. Serve with basmati rice, chapati (roti), or naan.

**Variations:**
**Aloo Matar**: Fry 2–3 chopped medium potatoes until golden brown and soft. Add to simmering curry instead of fried tofu cubes. **Rich & Creamy**: Blend tomatoes with 2–3 Tbs cashews and 1 Tbs tomato paste. For all variations, adjust water and salt as needed.

# Navratan Korma
## North Indian vegetables, fruit & nuts in cream sauce

serves 3 to 4 / time 60 min

**1 large (175 g) potato** peeled, chopped
**1/2 small head (150 g) cauliflower** chopped
**1 medium (80 g) carrot** peeled, chopped
**1 cup (115 g) green beans**
**1 cup (120 g) pineapple** chopped
**3/4 cup (90 g) peas**
**1/4 cup (30 g) almonds**
**1/4 cup (30 g) cashews**
**1/3 cup (40 g) golden raisins**

**2 Tbs vegetable oil**
**2 tsp cumin** ground
**2 tsp coriander** ground
**1 tsp Garam Masala**
**2 bay leaves**
**1 cinnamon stick**
**1 black cardamom pod**
**8–12 strands saffron**

**1 medium (70 g) onion** chopped
**3 cloves garlic** chopped
**1 in (3 cm) fresh ginger** chopped
**1 green chili** seeded, sliced *optional*
**2 Tbs (45 g) almonds**
**2 Tbs (45 g) cashews**
**1 Tbs white poppy seeds** or **cashews**
**3/4 cup (180 ml) water**

**1 cup (240 ml) soy cream** or **oat cream**
**1 1/4 cup (300 ml) water** more as needed
**1 tsp sugar**
**1 1/2 tsp salt** more as needed

1. Bring 1/4 cup (60 ml) **water** to boil in a pot. Add chopped **potato**, **cauliflower**, **carrot**, and **green beans**. Cover and steam undisturbed on low until mostly soft, 7-10 min. Remove from heat, cover, and set aside.

2. Heat 1 Tbs **oil** in a large pot on medium heat. Add chopped **onion**, **garlic**, **ginger**, and **green chili** (if using), 2 Tbs **almonds**, 2 Tbs **cashews**, and 1 Tbs **poppy seeds** (or **cashews**). Stir fry until aromatic, 3–5 min.

3. Transfer to a blender along with 3/4 cup (180 ml) **water** and blend on high until smooth.

4. Heat 1 Tbs **oil** in the pot on medium heat. Add **cumin**, **coriander**, **Garam Masala**, **bay leaves**, **cinnamon**, and **black cardamom**. Stir in blended paste. Cook until richly aromatic, stirring regularly, 5–8 min.

5. Stir in **soy** (or **oat**) **cream** and **saffron**. Simmer on low, gradually stir in another 1 cup (240 ml) **water**.

6. Gently stir in steamed potatoes, cauliflower, carrot, and green beans, followed by chopped **pineapple**, **peas**, 1/4 cup (30 g) **almonds**, 1/4 cup (30 g) **cashews**, and **raisins**, **sugar**, and **salt**.

7. Simmer on low, stirring often, adding water if needed, until vegetables are soft, 5–8 min. Remove from heat. Cover until ready to serve.

8. Serve with basmati rice, chapati (roti), or naan.

# Vegetable Jalfrezi
## North Indian spiced mixed vegetables

serves 2 to 3 / time 45 min

2 cups (180 g) **cauliflower** chopped
1 large (120 g) **carrot** peeled, chopped
2 medium large (200 g) **tomatoes** chopped
1 medium (200 g) **green** or **red pepper** chopped
1 1/2 cups (150 g) **green beans** and/or **peas**
1 medium (100 g) **onion** chopped
2–3 cloves **garlic** finely chopped
1 1/2 in (4 cm) **ginger** finely chopped
1–2 **green chilies** seeded, sliced *optional*

1/2 cup (120 ml) **soy yogurt**
1/4 cup (60 ml) **water** more as needed
1 Tbs **lemon juice**
1 tsp **rice vinegar**
1 tsp **sugar**
1 tsp **salt**
2 tsp **dried fenugreek leaves** for garnish

2–3 Tbs **vegetable oil**
1 tsp **black mustard seeds**
1 tsp **cumin** ground
1 tsp **coriander** ground
1/2 tsp **Garam Masala**
1/4 tsp **paprika** ground
1/2 tsp **turmeric** ground

1. Heat **oil** in a large pot or wok on medium heat. Add **mustard seeds**. After they start to pop (20–30 sec), add chopped **onion, garlic, ginger** and **green chili** (if using), followed by ground **cumin, coriander, Garam Masala, paprika**, and **turmeric**. Fry, stirring constantly, until richly aromatic, 2–3 min.

2. Add chopped **cauliflower** and **carrot**. Mix well. Stir fry until browned, 3–5 min.

3. Stir in chopped **tomatoes**. Fry until tomatoes start to fall apart, stirring often, another 3–5 min.

4. Add chopped **green** or **red peppers** and **green beans** or **peas**. Continue to cook, stirring often, just until peppers start to soften, 2–3 min.

5. In a bowl or cup, whisk **soy yogurt, water, lemon juice**, and **vinegar**. Gradually stir into sizzling vegetables.

6. Add **sugar** and **salt**. Mix well, bring to low boil and reduce heat to low. Simmer until sauce has thickened and vegetables are tender, another 5–7 min, stirring in slightly more water if needed. Remove from heat.

7. Garnish with **dried fenugreek leaves** and serve with basmati rice, naan, or chapati (roti).

**Variations:**
**Vedic**: Replace onion and garlic with 1/4 tsp asafoetida (hing). Add another chopped tomato with the others.
**Fruity**: Add 1/4 cup (30 g) golden raisins or chopped dates along with tomatoes. **Coconut**: Replace soy yogurt with coconut milk.

# Dal Makhani
## North Indian creamy black lentils & beans

serves 3 to 4 / time 90 min +

**1 cup (185 g) whole urid dal** (dried black lentils) or **3 cups (550 g) cooked black beans**
**1/3 cup (65 g) kidney beans** (dried) or **1 cup (180 g) cooked kidney beans**
**3–4 cups (720–1000 ml) water** more as needed

**2 large (250 g) tomatoes** chopped
**1 in (3 cm) fresh ginger** finely chopped
**3 cloves garlic** finely chopped *optional*
**1–2 green chilies** seeded, sliced *optional*

**2 Tbs vegetable oil**
**1 tsp black mustard seeds**
**2 bay leaves**
**1 cinnamon stick** or **1/4 tsp cinnamon** ground
**1 black cardamom pods** or **4 green cardamom pods**
**2 tsp cumin** ground
**1 tsp coriander** ground
**1/2 tsp red chili powder** or **paprika** (ground)
**1 tsp Garam Masala**
**1/4 tsp asafoetida** (hing)
**1 1/4 tsp salt**

**2 Tbs margarine**
**1 Tbs lemon juice**
**1 tsp sugar**
**1 cup (240 ml) soy cream** or **oat cream**
**small handful fresh coriander** chopped, for garnish

1. If using dried **whole urid dal** and **kidney beans**, rinse well and soak 8 hrs or overnight.
   Drain and discard soaking water. Add soaked dal, beans, and 4 cups (1000 ml) **water** to a large pot.
   Bring to boil and cook covered on low heat until soft, 1–2 hrs. Continue to simmer on low.

2. If using cooked (e.g. canned) **beans**, rinse and drain them, then add to a large pot along with
   3 cups (720 ml) **water**. Bring to simmer on low heat.

3. Purée chopped **tomatoes** in a blender or food processor. Stir into simmering lentils and/or beans.

4. Heat **oil** in a small pan on medium heat. Add **mustard seeds**. After they start to pop (20–30 sec),
   add chopped **ginger, garlic** and **green chilies** (if using), **bay leaves**, **cinnamon**, **cardamom**,
   ground **cumin**, **coriander**, **red chili powder** (or **paprika**), **Garam Masala**, and **asafoetida**.
   Fry, stirring constantly, until richly aromatic, 1–2 min.

5. Stir fried spices and oil from small pan into large pot of simmering lentils and/or beans.
   Simmer on low, mashing and stirring occasionally, 20–30 min, adding more **water** if needed.

6. Stir in **salt**, **margarine**, **lemon juice**, **sugar**, and most of the **soy** (or **oat**) **cream**, saving some for garnish.
   Continue to simmer on low, stirring occasionally, another 5–10 min. Remove from heat.

7. Drizzle with remaining **soy** (or **oat**) **cream** and garnish with chopped **fresh coriander**.

8. Serve with basmati rice, naan, or chapati (roti).

# Sindhi Bhindi Masala
## North Indian okra

serves 2 / time 30 min

**3 cups (7 oz / 250 g) okra**
**2 small (100 g) tomatoes** chopped
**1 small (75 g) onion** chopped *optional*
**2 cloves garlic** finely chopped *optional*
**1 green chili** seeded, sliced *optional*

**2 Tbs vegetable oil**
**1 tsp black mustard seeds**
**1 tsp cumin** ground
**1 tsp coriander** ground
**1/2 tsp Garam Masala**
**1/8 tsp asafoetida** (hing)
**1/4 tsp turmeric** ground
**1/2 cup (120 ml) water**
**1 Tbs chickpea flour** (besan)
**3/4 tsp salt**
**1 tsp lemon juice**
**1/2 tsp sugar**
**small handful fresh coriander** chopped, for garnish

1. Rinse and dry **okra**. Cut and discard ends and tips (1/2 in / 1 cm each side). Slice into 1 in (3 cm) pieces.
2. Heat **oil** in a medium pot or pan on medium heat. Add **mustard seeds**. After they start to pop (20–30 sec), add chopped **onion**, **garlic**, and **chili** (if using), followed by ground **cumin**, **coriander**, Garam Masala, and **asafoetida**. Fry, stirring regularly, until richly aromatic and onions begin to soften, 2–4 min.
3. Add chopped okra, **tomatoes**, and **turmeric**. Fry, stirring regularly, until tomatoes fall apart, 4–5 min. Add a bit of water and reduce heat if needed.
4. Stir in 1/4 cup (60 ml) **water**, **chickpea flour**, and **salt**. Continue to cook on medium low heat, gradually stirring in remaining 1/4 cup (60 ml) **water**, until okra are mostly soft and sauce has thickened, 8–12 min.
5. Stir in **sugar** and **lemon juice**. Remove from heat.
6. Garnish with chopped **fresh coriander** and serve with basmati rice, naan, or chapati (roti).

# Bengan Bhartha
## North Indian roasted eggplant

serves 2 to 3 / time 45 min +

**2 medium (450 g) eggplants** (aubergines)
**2 small (150 g) tomatoes** chopped
**1 medium (100 g) onion** chopped
**3 cloves garlic** finely chopped
**3/4 in (2 cm) fresh ginger** finely chopped
**1 green chili** finely chopped *optional*
**small bunch fresh coriander** chopped

**3 Tbs vegetable oil** more as needed
**3/4 tsp black mustard seeds**
**3/4 tsp cumin** ground
**3/4 tsp coriander** ground
**1/2 tsp Garam Masala**
**1/4 tsp asafoetida** (hing) *optional*
**1/2 tsp turmeric** ground
**1/2 tsp amchoor (mango) powder** *optional*
**3–4 Tbs water** more as needed
**2 Tbs lemon juice**
**1 tsp salt**

1. Oven method: Preheat oven to 425°F / 220°C / level 7. Poke whole **eggplants** (aubergines) several times with a fork. Rub them with a bit of oil and roast them on the middle rack in oven until charred, shriveled, and soft, 40–60 min. Remove from oven. Set aside to cool for 5–10 min.

   Stove method: Roast **eggplants** whole, directly on a gas burner on a low flame, turning them regularly with tongs until outsides are charred and insides are soft and cooked, 10–15 min. Set aside to cool.

2. Cut off and discard stems and bottom ends of roasted eggplants. Slice in half lengthwise, scoop out cooked, soft insides into a bowl and discard outer peels.

3. Heat **oil** in a large frying pan or wok on medium heat. Add **mustard seeds**. After they start to pop (20–30 sec), add chopped **onion, garlic, ginger, green chili** (if using), ground **cumin, coriander, Garam Masala,** and **asafoetida** (if using). Fry, stirring often, until richly aromatic and onions are browned, 3–5 min.

4. Add cooked eggplants, chopped **tomatoes**, ground **turmeric**, and **amchoor powder** (if using). Mix well. Fry, stirring regularly, adding water gradually as needed until sauce thickens, darkens, and oil separates, about 10–15 min. Remove from heat.

5. Stir in **lemon juice**, **salt**, and most of chopped **fresh coriander**.

6. Garnish with remaining chopped **coriander**. Serve with Naan (page 144), chapati (roti), or basmati rice.

**Variations:**
**Vedic**: Replace chopped garlic and onion with another small chopped tomato.

# Chilli Paneer
## Indo-Chinese sweet & sour tofu

serves 2 / time 45 min

**tofu paneer:**
- 7 oz (200 g) tofu
- 2 Tbs lemon juice
- 1 Tbs soy sauce
- 2 Tbs nutritional yeast flakes or chickpea flour (besan)
- 2 Tbs corn starch
- 2–3 Tbs coconut oil or vegetable oil

1. Cut **tofu** in slabs and wrap in a dish towel. Weight with a cutting board for 15–20 min to remove excess moisture. Unwrap and cut into triangles or cubes
2. Combine **lemon juice**, **soy sauce**, **nutritional yeast flakes** (or **chickpea flour**), and **corn starch** in bowl. Add tofu cubes, mix well, coat all pieces.
3. Heat **oil** in a small frying pan on medium high. Fry battered cubes in batches until evenly golden brown, turning regularly, 4–6 min. Remove, drain, set aside.

**vegetables & sauce:**

- 2 medium (150 g) **tomatoes** chopped
- 1/2 medium (90 g) **red pepper** chopped
- 1/2 medium (80 g) **green pepper** chopped
- 2/3 cup (100 g) **fresh pineapple** chopped
- 1 medium (120 g) **onion** chopped
- 2 cloves **garlic** finely chopped
- 1 in (3 cm) **fresh ginger** finely chopped
- 1–2 green **chilies** seeded, sliced

- 2–3 **spring onions** chopped, for garnish

- 2 Tbs **vegetable oil**
- 1/2 tsp **black mustard seeds**
- 1 tsp **coriander** ground
- 1/2 tsp **black pepper** ground
- 1 tsp **paprika** ground
- 1/4 tsp **turmeric** ground
- 1 Tbs **lemon juice** or **2 tsp rice vinegar**
- 1 Tbs **sugar**
- 1/2 cup (120 ml) **water**
- 1 Tbs **soy sauce**
- 1 Tbs **corn starch**
- 1/2 tsp **salt**

1. Heat **oil** in a large pan or wok on medium high heat. Add **mustard seeds**. After they start to pop (20–30 sec), add chopped **onion**, **garlic**, **ginger**, **green chilies**, ground **black pepper**, **coriander**, **paprika**, and **turmeric**. Fry while stirring until richly aromatic, 2–3 min.
2. Add chopped **tomatoes**, **red** and **green peppers**, **pineapple**, **lemon juice** (or **rice vinegar**), and **sugar**. Stir-fry on medium heat until tomatoes fall apart and peppers and pineapple are scorched, 4–6 min.
3. Whisk **water** and **soy sauce** with **corn starch** in a bowl. Gradually pour mixture into sizzling vegetables while stirring. Stir in **salt** and cook, stirring constantly, until sauce thickens, 2–3 min.
4. Stir in fried tofu cubes and coat them with sauce. Simmer on low heat, stirring regularly, another 2–3 min.
5. Garnish with chopped **spring onions** and serve with rice.

**Variations:**
**Vedic:** Replace chopped onion and garlic with 1/4 tsp asafoetida (hing) and 1/2 tsp Garam Masala, followed by another chopped small tomato along with red and green peppers.

# Vegetable Manchurian
## Indo-Chinese dumplings

serves 2 to 3 / time 45 min

**dumplings:**

**1 1/2 cups (160 g) cabbage** shredded / chopped
**1 large (120 g) carrot** grated
**2/3 cup (90 g) flour** (all-purpose / type 550)
**2 Tbs corn starch**
**1/4 tsp turmeric** ground
**1/2 tsp ajwain** or **dried thyme**
**1/2 tsp salt**
**1/4 cup (60 ml) water**
**vegetable oil** for frying

1. Toss shredded **cabbage** and grated **carrot** in a mixing bowl with **flour**, **corn starch**, ground **turmeric**, **ajwain** (or **thyme**), and **salt**.
2. Gradually add **water** and combine well to form a sticky, clumpy batter.
3. Heat 1–2 in (3–5 cm) **oil** in a small pot on medium high heat. The oil is hot enough when a small bit of batter sizzles and rises to the surface immediately.
4. Form batter into walnut-sized pieces with damp hands. (If batter is too wet, mix in some more corn starch. If it's too dry and pieces fall apart, add slightly more water.) Drop 5 to 6 pieces into hot oil quickly, but carefully. Do not crowd the oil. Fry, turning regularly, until dark golden brown, 4–6 minutes.
5. Drain and transfer fried dumplings with a slotted spoon to a plate as they finish. Fry another batch or two of dumplings until batter is done.

**sauce:**

**1/2 cup (55 g) cabbage** chopped
**2 medium (160 g) tomatoes** chopped
**1 medium (90 g) red onion** chopped
**1–2 cloves garlic** finely chopped
**1 in (3 cm) fresh ginger** finely chopped
**1 green chili** chopped *optional*
**2–3 spring onions** chopped, for garnish

**1 Tbs vegetable oil**
**1/2 tsp black mustard seeds**
**1/2 tsp coriander ground**
**1/2 tsp black pepper** ground
**1/4 cup (60 ml) soy sauce**
**1 Tbs lemon juice** or **2 tsp rice vinegar**
**1 1/4 cup (300 ml) water**
**1 Tbs corn starch**
**1 Tbs sugar**

1. Heat **oil** in a medium sauce pan on medium heat. Add **mustard seeds**. After they start to pop (20–30 sec), add chopped **onion**, **garlic**, **ginger**, **green chili** (if using), ground **coriander**, and **black pepper**. Fry, stirring constantly, until richly aromatic, 2–3 min.
2. Stir in chopped **cabbage** and **tomatoes**. Continue to stir fry until tomatoes fall apart, 3–5 minutes.
3. Whisk **soy sauce**, **lemon juice** (or **rice vinegar**), and **water** with **corn starch** and **sugar**. Gradually stir into sizzling vegetables. Bring to simmer. Reduce heat to low. Cook until thickened, 2–3 min.
4. Add fried dumplings to thickened, simmering sauce. Mix gently to cover all pieces. Continue to simmer on low heat, partially covered, another 2–3 min. Remove from heat.
5. Garnish with chopped **spring onions**. Serve as an appetizer or with steamed rice.

# Halva
## Indian semolina sweet

serves 4 / time 30 min

**1 3/4 cups (420 ml) water**
**1/2 in (1 cm) fresh ginger** sliced
**1 cinnamon stick** or **1/2 tsp cinnamon** ground
**5 green cardamom pods** crushed
**5 cloves**
**1/2 tsp nutmeg** ground
**1 tsp orange zest** or **lemon zest** *optional*
**4 saffron threads** *optional*
**2/3 cup (135 g) sugar**

**1/3 cup (75 g) margarine**
**2/3 cup (125 g) fine semolina**
**1/4 cup (30 g) almonds** or **cashews**
**1/3 cup (40 g) raisins**

1. Bring **water** to boil in small pot. Add sliced **ginger**, **cinnamon**, **cardamom**, **cloves**, **nutmeg**, and **orange** or **lime zest** (if using). Reduce heat to low and simmer gently for 7–8 min.

2. Strain simmering spice water into another small pot and discard the whole spices. Transfer the strained spice water back into the small pot and return to simmer on low heat.

3. Add **saffron** (if using) and **sugar**. Stir gently until sugar dissolves to form a light and thin syrup, 1–2 min. Remove from heat.

4. Heat **margarine** in a large pan or pot on medium low heat. Gradually add **semolina** while stirring. Mix thoroughly and turn with a wooden spatula or spoon. Toast the grains stirring constantly until they absorb all of the oil, are lightly toasted and golden brown, 7–10 minutes. Do not overcook or burn them!

5. Stir in **almonds** (or **cashews**) and **raisins** (and/or ingredients in Variations, below). Reduce heat to low.

6. Pour spice syrup gradually into the pan with cooked semolina, stirring constantly.

7. Continue to stir constantly, cook uncovered until liquid is absorbed and texture becomes fluffy, 7–10 min. Remove from heat.

8. Cover for 5–10 min before serving.

## Variations:
**Berry Halva**: Use 1/2 cup (60 g) fresh or frozen blueberries, raspberries, or strawberries instead of raisins.
**Carrot Walnut Halva**: Add 1 small (40 g) grated carrot and crumbled walnuts instead of almonds or cashews.
**Chocolate/Carob Halva**: Gently stir in a handful of carob or chocolate chips in the final minutes of cooking. Optionally, add 1 Tbs cocoa or carob powder along with nuts. Omit saffron and zest for variations if desired.

# Saffron Mango Lassi
## Indian yogurt shake

serves 2 / time 15 min +

- **1 small (125 g) mango** (fresh or frozen) chopped
- **2/3 cup (160 ml) water** more as needed
- **2–3 Tbs sugar**
- **6–8 saffron threads** more as needed
- **1 cup (220 g) soy yogurt** or **coconut yogurt**
- **6–8 ice cubes**
- **1/4 tsp rose water** *optional*
- **2–3 green cardamom pods** crushed or **1/8 tsp cardamom** ground *optional*

1. Bring 1/3 cup (80 ml) **water** to boil in a small pot on low heat. Add **sugar** and stir until mostly dissolved. Remove from heat. Stir in **saffron** threads. Let cool 20–30 min.

2. In a blender, combine chopped **mango**, **yogurt**, **ice cubes**, **rose water**, and **cardamom** (if using). Blend at gradually increasing speed until mostly smooth.

3. Add cooled saffron syrup and remaining 1/3 cup (80 ml) **water**. Continue to blend until smooth, adding slightly more cold **water** or **sugar** as desired.

4. Pour into chilled glasses and garnish with a few **saffron threads** and serve, or transfer to the fridge and chill for 1–2 hrs before serving.

## Variations:
**Banana Lassi**: Omit saffron. Replace mango with 1–2 small, chopped bananas. **Jeera Lassi**: Skip step one. Omit mango, saffron, sugar, rose water, and cardamom. Instead, add 1/8 tsp salt and 1/2 tsp ground cumin, adjusted to taste. Blend with cold water. Optionally, garnish with a drizzle of 1/2 tsp tamarind paste whisked with 2–3 tsp palm or agave syrup.

# Naan
## North Indian flatbread

makes 2 to 3 pieces / time 30 min +

**1/2 tsp dry active yeast**
**1/2 tsp sugar**
**3 Tbs warm water**
**1 1/2 cups (200 g) flour** (all-purpose / type 550)
**1/2 tsp salt**
**3 Tbs soy yogurt** or **coconut yogurt**
**2 Tbs vegetable oil**
**1 tsp kalonji (nigella) seeds** or **black poppy seeds**
**1 Tbs margarine** *optional*
**fresh coriander** chopped, for garnish

1. Whisk **yeast** and **sugar** with 3 Tbs warm (not hot) water in a small bowl. Cover and let sit 5 min.
2. Combine **flour** and **salt** in a large bowl.
3. Add **yeast**, **sugar**, and **water** to bowl with flour. Add **soy** (or **coconut**) **yogurt** and 2 Tbs **oil**. Mix and knead 5–7 min to form a soft, rubbery dough. If dough is too sticky, add slightly more flour. If dough is dry, add just a bit of water. Cover and let rise in a warm place 1–2 hrs.
4. Preheat oven to 500°F / 260°C / level 10.
5. Separate dough into 2 or 3 pieces. Briefly knead each and then roll out (with a rolling pin) or press and stretch to make flat ovals about 1/4 in (5 mm) thick. Transfer to a pizza stone or baking tray.
6. Sprinkle **kalonji** or **black poppy seeds** over each naan.
7. Place pizza stone or baking tray on middle rack of oven and bake until golden brown, 5–8 min.
8. Move to top rack and bake until toasted with some dark spots, another 2–3 min. Remove from oven.
9. Optionally, spread **margarine** on each naan.
10. Cover or wrap baked naan in a kitchen towel to keep warm and soft until ready to serve.
11. Garnish with chopped fresh coriander before serving.

## Variations:
**Stove-Top**: Instead of baking in the oven, grill flatbreads in a large, heavy frying pan (without oil) until golden brown with dark spots, 3–5 min on each side. **Garlic Naan**: Combine 1–2 cloves of finely chopped garlic with 1 Tbs vegetable oil in a small bowl. Spread mixture over flatbreads before sprinkling with kalonji (or poppy seeds) and baking (or grilling) as above.

# Haldi Chawal
## North Indian golden rice with turmeric

serves 2 / time 20 min +

**1 cup (185 g) basmati rice**
**1 Tbs vegetable oil**
**1/2 tsp black mustard seeds**
**1/2 tsp turmeric** ground
**2 green cardamom pods**
**2 cloves**
**1/2 tsp salt**
**1 2/3 cups (400 ml) water**

1. Rinse and drain **rice** thoroughly. If desired, soak the rice in cold water for 20 min. Drain, discard water.
2. Heat **oil** in a small pot on medium heat. Add **mustard seeds**. After they start to pop (20–30 sec), add rice, **turmeric**, **cardamom**, **cloves**, and **salt**. Stir several times and lightly toast rice for 30 sec.
3. Stir in 1 2/3 cup (400 ml) **water**. Bring to boil. Reduce heat to low. Cover and cook undisturbed 15–20 min.
4. Remove cover. Mix gently a few times with a fork. Cover and allow to absorb remaining moisture, 5–10 min.
5. Remove and discard cardamom pods and cloves before serving.

# Jeera Pulao
## North Indian rice with cumin seeds

serves 2 / time 20 min +

**1 cup (185 g) basmati rice**
**1 Tbs vegetable oil**
**1 tsp cumin seeds** (whole)
**1 small cinnamon stick**
**1 black cardamom pod**
**1 bay leaf**
**1/2 tsp salt**
**1 2/3 cups (400 ml) water**

1. Rinse and drain **rice** thoroughly. Optionally, soak rice in cold water for 20 min. Drain, discard water.
2. Heat **oil** in a small pot on medium heat. Add **cumin seeds**. Fry until richly aromatic, about 20–30 sec. Add rice, **cinnamon**, **cardamom**, **bay leaf**, and **salt**. Stir several times and cook for 30 sec.
3. Stir in 1 2/3 cup (400 ml) **water**. Bring to boil. Reduce heat to low. Cover and cook undisturbed 15–20 min.
4. Remove cover. Mix gently a few times with a fork. Cover and allow to absorb remaining moisture, 5–10 min.
5. Remove and discard cinnamon stick, cardamom pod, and bay leaf before serving.

# Narayal Chawal
## South Asian coconut rice

serves 2 / time 30 min

> **1 cup (185 g) jasmine** or **basmati rice**
> **1 2/3 cups (400 ml) water**
> **1/2 cup (120 ml) coconut milk**
> **2 pandan leaves** or **bay leaves**
> **1/2 tsp salt**

1. Rinse and drain **rice** thoroughly. Optionally, soak rice in cold water for 20 min. Drain, discard water.
2. Bring 1 2/3 cup (400 ml) **water** to boil in a small pot. Stir in rice, **coconut milk**, **pandan** or **bay leaves**, and **salt**.
3. Return to boil and reduce heat to low. Cover and cook undisturbed for 20–25 min. Turn off heat.
4. Uncover and mix gently a few times with a fork. Cover and allow to absorb remaining moisture, 5–10 min.
5. Remove and discard pandan or bay leaves before serving.


# Do Chua
## Vietnamese pickled radish

makes about 1 cup (200 g) / time 15 min +

> **1 small (100 g) daikon / white radish** peeled, thinly sliced
> or **5–6 small (100 g) red radishes** thinly sliced
> **1/3 cup (80 ml) rice vinegar**
> **1/3 cup (80 ml) boiling hot water**
> **2 Tbs sugar**
> **2 tsp salt**

1. If using **white radish** or **radish** with thick skins, first peel and discard skins before slicing. With small **red radishes**, leave the peels on for the pinkish tint.
2. Combine **all ingredients** in a jar. Shake well until sugar and salt fully dissolve.
3. Cover loosely. Set aside and let sit and cool 1–2 hrs.
4. Close jar well and transfer to the fridge. Ideally chill and marinate 2–3 days. Keeps in fridge 3–4 weeks.
5. Chop finely for Pad Thai (page 85) or use slices for Bánh Mì (page 93). Add 1–2 Tbs of liquid to Southeast Asian sauces or noodle and rice dishes for extra flavor.

# AFRICA

THE LOTUS AND THE ARTICHOKE

# AFRICA

### Curry on the Coast
### Mombasa, Kenya. 05/2000

The boy driving the matatu van was at most 13. He literally could only reach the pedals because wooden blocks were attached to them. He drove the battered vehicle like a race car, squeezing through the most impossible gaps in traffic, veering sharply to the sides of the road, skidding to a momentary halt so passengers could climb in. As soon as additional riders had a few limbs inside the vehicle, the engine would roar and we'd roll off and everyone would shift about and pull the new occupants in. Every time I thought there was no way anyone else could possibly fit, we'd stop at another crowd at the curb, the sliding door would open, and more bodies would pack in. It was truly incredible! It was also unbelievably hot, loud, and dusty.

I was sitting on V's lap with two Maasai warriors (in regal red plaid, clutching their spears) pressed tightly beside us, an elderly nun on my right, and a couple guys in worn-out business attire perched on the end of the bench seat. With every swerve, every bump, we moved in unison, gripping each other, gasping, and then chuckling at every close call.

Through the mass of bodies, fashions, weapons, luggage, and a mostly shattered windscreen, I sighted the sign of the restaurant: Island Dishes! I waved my arms and shouted to the doorman. He banged twice on the van's ceiling to alert the driver of an intended stop. He grabbed the wrinkled currency from my outstretched fingers with one hand and threw open the door with the other. On cue, hands pushed and pulled us until we were out the door and almost standing before the van launched back into the chaotic traffic.

Yesterday's Red Curry was outstanding, but today I was determined to try something new: the Biryani. It, too, was an explosion of flavors and culinary collisions.

### Washed in Blue
### Chefchaouen, Morocco. 07/2004

*Petit déjeuner* every morning on the roof – fresh orange juice, toasted bread with jam, black coffee, a paperback novel and my sketchbook. Singing birds, buzzing insects, the chatter of the streets below. The houses are all washed in blue. It's sunny and bright. A crisp mountain breeze brings the bed sheets on clotheslines to life.

It's a million times more relaxed here than Fès! So much energy there: Mad motorbikes in the mazes of the medina, blue-eyed boys guiding me back to Bab Bou Jeloud, others determined to sell me kif, slippers, or carpets. The sensory overload of the souks. Hot and loud all day, hungry and lonely at night – looking for more than another tajine or couscous.

I've chased the ghosts of Bowles and Burroughs in Tangier. Dined at dusk at Marrakesh's monstrous Djemaa el-Fnaa. Drove to Ouarzazate and Gorges du Dadés with Sebastiano in a rented Renault. Explored crumbling casbahs, lunched at local eateries in little towns, and had midnight picnics. So, so many stars!

### The Bad Luck Boy
### Luxor, Egypt. 10/2007

Slept all of about an hour last night but I feel fantastic and alive. Met Naveen and Maik at Salt & Bread for a late dinner: ta'ameya and mesa'ah with pita. It's a good thing I could eat Egyptian fava bean and aubergine dishes all day every day, because that's pretty much what I've been doing for the past week. After dinner we ordered countless rounds of mint tea and apple sisha, and played backgammon until 4 a.m.

We decided to stay up for the sunrise so we walked back to my guesthouse and took the stairs to the roof. The sun came up. Ahmed brought us black coffee, fresh bread, and fruit from the kitchen. I went downstairs for a short rest and then a cold shower.

Naveen and I took the ferry across the Nile, but Maik stayed back— he had some trouble with his eye, but perhaps he's tired – or nervous. Naveen told us stories of being attacked and robbed in Iraq, scuffles in Lebanon and Syria, and sneaking across borders all over the Middle East without entry visas. Yeah, I could've chosen a better travel companion for the day. Wildly entertaining, but not exactly the guy I'd invite on a high stakes expedition. I figured renting bikes and checking out some ancient tombs would be okay.

I must be most of the 8 km from the river to the Valley of the Kings. Naveen is somewhere behind me in a village around the curve and beyond the steep hill I just crossed. Twenty minutes ago we stopped to take photographs. A group of children rushed to greet us. All was well until two men with automatic assault rifles came out of a house. They shouted angrily and didn't look pleased to see us. I told Naveen repeatedly we should go, but he wouldn't put his camera away. The men continued yelling and began to run towards us, gripping their guns. I insisted again that we leave. Immediately. He laughed and waved his hand, inviting me to flee. I thought briefly of his many "unlucky" incidents, and then I quickly pedaled away from the scene. I don't know where he is now, or why he hasn't caught up.

I'll wait another half hour here in the shade before moving on.

## Seven Seater
**Dakar, Senegal. 10/2009**

Got up at the call to worship. The muezzin's electric voice singing through the alleys and into the open windows of my little room at Saint-Louis Sun Hotel. Cold shower and out the door. Abdou drove me to *Gare Routiere Pompiers*, an absolute circus of a station an hour's urban safari from where we began.

It was a challenge, swimming in a sea of shouting drivers and riders intent on filling rundown Renaults and Peugeots for overland journeys to every corner of Senegal within a day's drive. Eventually I found the vehicles bound for Banjul, The Gambia. Drank a sweet coffee at a makeshift stall while the driver tied a dozen bulky pieces of luggage to the roof with ropes. The engine doesn't want to start, but then it does.

Thirty minutes on, our car grinds to a halt and dies. Now we're on the side of the road in the already hot, still hectic outskirts of Dakar.

The driver says another *Sept-Place* will rescue us in an hour. Maybe two. *Inshallah.* So we're all squatting in the shade in silence. Calm and unfazed. No one is anxious or angry. There is no rush. This happens all the time.

Ninety minutes later another battered Renault seven-seater taxi pulls up; Red dust swirls around us. Brief chatter. In no particular hurry we stand up, leisurely load up our new ride, climb into our busted seats and continue the six hour bumpy journey to the border.

## Finding Fela
**Lagos, Nigeria. 10/2014**

I awoke to the sound of rain falling and the low hum of air conditioners and rumbling power generators of the Parkview Astoria hotel. Power cuts, gray skies, a stray mosquito buzzing around the room. Nothing can bring me down – I'm excited to be here, and thrilled to be doing cooking shows and kicking out a 5-course dinner party tomorrow night with Chef Tiyan. On Saturday there's a fashion show. Sunday we're going to a stage play reenacting the life and music of Fela Kuti. It's gonna be wild.

Last night and this morning I swam in the small, tiled pool. I'm like a kid; If I'm anywhere with a pool I have to swim in it two or three times a day. It's a treat to stay somewhere this fancy. Certainly not my usual style, but Bernd insisted we get rooms at a place with a pool. I was happy to accept.

Breakfast was amusing: Fresh fruit sliced in funny shapes, baked beans, and toasted white bread with jam. Served on a plate wrapped in plastic. I hung out with the crew in the kitchen and had another coffee in the bar.

Really looking forward to lunch again at Hakeem's restaurant: traditional Nigerian food with his family and friends has been awesome, so many dishes they've always known – but all so new to me.

# Plasas & Fufu
## Gambian spinach peanut stew with mashed cassava

serves 2 to 3 / time 35 min

**plasas (spinach peanut stew):**
   **8–10 cups (12 oz / 350 g) spinach** chopped
   **1 large (230 g) sweet potato** peeled, chopped
   **2 medium (160 g) tomatoes** chopped
   **1 medium (100 g) red onion** chopped
   **2 cloves garlic** finely chopped
   **1/2 tsp black pepper** ground

   **2 Tbs vegetable oil**
   **3 Tbs peanut butter** or **peanuts** lightly roasted, ground
   **1–2 Tbs tomato paste**
   **2 tsp vegetable broth powder**
   **1/2 tsp salt**
   **3/4 cup (180 ml) water**
   **1/4 cup (30 g) peanuts** lightly roasted, for garnish

1. Heat 2 Tbs **oil** in large pot on medium heat.
2. Add chopped **onion**, **garlic**, and ground **black pepper**. Fry, stirring regularly, until aromatic. 2–3 min.
3. Add chopped **sweet potato** and **tomatoes**. Cook until tomatoes fall apart, 4–6 min, stirring regularly.
4. In a bowl or measuring cup, whisk **peanut butter** (or ground peanuts), **tomato paste**, **vegetable broth powder**, **salt**, and **water**. Stir into pot. Bring to low boil, reduce heat to medium low. Simmer partially covered, stirring occasionally, 10 min.
5. Stir in chopped **spinach**. Cover and steam 5–7 min, stirring occasionally, adding more water if needed. When the spinach is done, stir a few times and turn off heat.
6. Garnish with roasted **peanuts**. Serve with fufu or rice.

**fufu (mashed cassava):**
   **18 oz (500 g) cassava** (also known as: manioc & yuca) peeled, chopped
   **1 Tbs margarine** or **vegetable oil**
   **1 1/2 cup (360 ml) water** more as needed
   **1/4 tsp salt**

1. Bring 1 1/2 cup (360 ml) **water** to boil in large pot. Add chopped **cassava**.
2. Return to boil, reduce heat to low. Cover, steam until soft, stirring occasionally, about 20 min.
3. Remove from heat. Add **margarine** (or oil) and **salt**. Mix well. Let cool 5–10 min.
4. Blend or mash until mostly smooth with an immersion blender or potato masher until mostly smooth. Add water gradually, if needed. The consistency should be similar to thick, sticky mashed potatoes.

# Dabo Firfir
## Ethiopian bread in Berbere tomato sauce

serves 2 / time 35 min

**3–4 large slices (200 g) stale bread** chopped (e.g. sourdough, baguette, etc.)
**4 small (200 g) plum tomatoes** chopped
**1 medium (100 g) red onion** finely chopped
**2 cloves garlic** finely chopped
**1/2 in (1 cm) fresh ginger** finely chopped

**3/4 cup (180 ml) water** more as needed
**2 Tbs vegetable oil**
**1 Tbs olive oil**
**2 tsp Berbere** spice mix
**1 tsp paprika** ground
**1/2 tsp black pepper** ground
**1/4 tsp turmeric** ground
**2 Tbs tomato paste**
**5–6 soft dates** chopped
**3 Tbs white wine** *optional*
**2 Tbs lemon juice**
**2 tsp sugar**
**3/4 tsp salt**
**1 small green jalapeño** seeded, sliced *optional*

1. Purée chopped **tomatoes** with 1/2 cup (120 ml) **water** in a small food processor or blender. Set aside.
2. Heat **vegetable oil** and **olive oil** in a large pot on medium low heat. Add chopped **onions**, **garlic**, and **ginger**. Fry until onions are soft, stirring frequently, 8–12 min.
3. Stir in **Berbere**, ground **paprika**, **black pepper**, and **turmeric**. Mix well and fry another 1–2 min.
4. Stir in puréed tomatoes, **tomato paste**, chopped **dates, wine** (if using), **lemon juice**, **sugar**, and **salt**.
5. Bring to simmer and reduce heat to medium low. Simmer until deep red and thickened, gradually stirring in another 1/4 cup (60 ml) **water**, or more as needed, 15–20 min.
6. Add chopped **bread**. Gently stir pieces into the sauce until well coated. Remove from heat.
7. Garnish with sliced **jalapeño** (if using) and serve.

### Variations:
**Injera Firfir:** If you can get or make them, go more traditional with 1 or 2 Ethiopian injera flatbreads, chopped or ripped into pieces instead of stale bread. Also works great with day-old pancakes!
**Spinach Bedinich Firfir:** Add 2 medium (200 g) chopped potatoes along with spices. Fry until mostly soft, 8–10 min, before adding tomato purée. Stir in 2 cups (100 g) fresh chopped spinach for last 5 min of simmering, before adding chopped bread. Adjust salt as needed.

# Koshary
## Egyptian pasta, lentils & rice with red sauce & fried onions

serves 3 to 4 / time 60 min

### red sauce:
- 4–5 medium (400 g) **tomatoes** chopped
- 1 1/2 cups (360 ml) **water** more as needed
- 1 small (80 g) **onion** chopped
- 3 cloves **garlic** chopped
- 1 small **red chili** chopped *optional*
- 2 Tbs **vegetable oil**
- 1 tsp **cumin** ground
- 1 tsp **coriander** ground
- 1/2 tsp **black pepper** ground
- 1/2 tsp **paprika** ground
- 1/4 tsp **cinnamon** ground
- 1 tsp **sugar**
- 2 Tbs **vinegar**
- 2 Tbs **tomato paste**
- 3/4 tsp **salt**

### pasta, lentils & rice:
- 1 1/2 cups (150 g) **macaroni**
- 1/2 cup (90 g) **brown lentils** (dried)
- 1 cup (185 g) **rice**
- 1/2 tsp **salt**
- 2 1/4 cups (540 ml) **water**

### fried onions & toppings:
- 1 large (120 g) **onion** thinly sliced
- 2 Tbs **flour**
- 2 Tbs **vegetable oil**
- 1 1/2 cups (150 g) **chickpeas** (cooked)
- **fresh parsley** chopped, for garnish

1. In a blender, purée chopped **tomatoes** with 1 cup (240 ml) **water**.

2. Heat 2 Tbs **oil** in a medium pot on medium heat.

3. Add chopped **onion** and fry, stirring regularly, for 2–3 min. Add chopped **garlic** and **red chili** (if using). Continue to fry until onions are soft, another 2–3 min.

4. Stir in ground **cumin**, **coriander**, **black pepper**, **paprika**, and **cinnamon**. Mix well.

5. Add blended tomatoes, **sugar**, **vinegar**, **tomato paste**, and 3/4 tsp **salt**. Bring to boil, reduce heat to medium low. Simmer, gradually adding remaining 1/2 cup (120 ml) **water** (more if needed) until sauce is dark red, richly aromatic, and thickened, 15–20 min. Cover and set aside.

6. Boil **macaroni** (or other pasta) according to package instructions, stirring occasionally, about 10–12 min. Drain and set aside.

7. Rinse and drain lentils thoroughly. Cook until mostly soft in a pot of boiling water, about 10 min. Drain and discard water.

8. Rinse and drain **rice** well. Bring 2 1/4 cups (540 ml) **water** to boil in a medium pot. Add rice, partially cooked lentils, and **salt**. Return to boil. Cover and simmer on low heat until water is absorbed, 15–20 min. Remove from heat. Stir a few times. Cover and let sit 5–10 min to absorb any remaining moisture.

9. Warm cooked chickpeas in a small pot, adding a bit of water or oil, if desired. Cover and set aside.

10. Toss sliced **onions** in a bowl with **flour** until well coated.

11. Heat **oil** in a medium frying pan on medium heat. Add onion slices carefully to hot oil, first tapping off excess flour. Fry until browned and crispy, but not burnt, stirring often, 5–10 min.

12. Portion rice and lentils onto plates. Top with cooked pasta, red sauce, warmed chickpeas, fried onions, and chopped, fresh **parsley**. Serve.

# Tajine
## Moroccan vegetable stew

serves 3 to 4 / time 80 min

**1 medium (200 g) zucchini** or **squash** chopped
**2 medium (150 g) carrots** peeled, chopped
**1 large (200 g) potato** peeled, chopped
**1 medium (100 g) sweet potato** peeled, chopped
**20 small (300 g) cherry tomatoes** chopped
**3 shallots** or **2 small (160 g) red onions** chopped
**3 cloves garlic** finely chopped
**1 in (3 cm) fresh ginger** finely chopped
**1–2 red chilies** seeded, sliced *optional*
**1 cup (200 g) chickpeas** (cooked)
**4 dates** chopped
**6 dried apricots** chopped
**2 prunes** chopped
**3 Tbs olive oil**
**2 Tbs Ras el Hanout** spice mix (for homemade, see below)
**2 Tbs lemon juice**
**2 tsp lemon zest**
**1 1/4 tsp salt**
**small handful fresh parsley** chopped
**small handful fresh mint** chopped
**small handful fresh coriander** chopped

1. Heat **olive oil** in a large pot on medium high heat.
2. Add chopped **shallots** (or **red onions**), **garlic**, **ginger**, and **red chilies**. Fry until aromatic, about 3–5 min.
3. Add **Ras el Hanout** (or spices, see below) and stir well. Fry another 1–2 min until shallots (or onions) begin to brown and soften.
4. Stir in chopped **tomatoes**. Fry, stirring often until tomatoes start to fall apart, 5–7 min.
5. Add chopped **zucchini** (or **squash**), **carrots**, **potato**, **sweet potato**. Mix well.
6. Stir in cooked **chickpeas**, chopped **dates**, **apricots**, and **prunes**.
7. Stir in **lemon juice** and **zest**, and **salt**.
8. Lastly, mix in chopped **parsley**, **mint**, and **coriander**.
9. Transfer to a lightly greased dutch oven, traditional tajine, or covered casserole dish.
10. Preheat oven to 400° F / 200° C / level 6. Bake until vegetables are soft and scorched, and stew is bubbly, 30–40 min. Alternately, stir in 3–4 Tbs water, cover pot and simmer undisturbed on low heat for 25–35 min.
11. Serve with bread or steamed couscous.

## Variations:
**Ras el Hanout**: To make your own, in a small pan, lightly roast 2 tsp coriander seeds, 1/2 tsp cumin seeds, 1/2 tsp black peppercorns, 1/4 cinnamon stick, 1 cardamom pod, and 2 cloves. Grind roasted spices and mix with 2 tsp ground paprika, 3/4 tsp turmeric and 1/4 tsp nutmeg. If you have all of these spices already ground, you could just add these spices in place of Ras el Hanout.

# Mombasa Red Curry
## with tofu, sweet potato, pineapple & peanuts

serves 4 / time 45 min

**7 oz (200 g) firm tofu**
**1 medium large (220 g) sweet potato** peeled, chopped
**1 1/2 cups (100 g) green beans** chopped
**1 cup (125 g) pineapple** chopped
**1 medium (100 g) tomato** chopped
**2 Tbs dried apricots** chopped
**2 shallots** or **1 medium (100 g) red onion** chopped
**3 cloves garlic** finely chopped
**1 in (3 cm) ginger** finely chopped
**1 stalk lemongrass** finely chopped *optional*
**1 red chili** seeded, sliced *optional*
**2 Tbs vegetable oil**
**2 tsp coriander** ground
**1 tsp cumin** ground
**1 tsp paprika** ground
**1/2 tsp turmeric** ground
**1/2 cinnamon stick** or **1/4 tsp cinnamon** ground
**1 black cardamom pod** or **2 green cardamom pods**
**2 bay leaves**
**1 2/3 cups (400 ml) coconut milk**
**1/2 cup (120 ml) water** more as needed
**1 Tbs lime juice**
**1 tsp salt**
**1/3 cup (45 g) peanuts** lightly roasted
**small handful fresh basil** or **parsley** chopped, for garnish

1. Cut **tofu** in slabs, wrap in a kitchen towel. Weight with a heavy cutting board and press out extra moisture, 15–20 min. Unwrap and cut in medium cubes.

2. Heat **oil** in a large pot on medium high heat. Add chopped **shallots** (or **onion**). Fry, stirring regularly, until lightly browned, 2–3 min. Add **tofu** cubes and chopped **sweet potato**. Continue to fry another 5–6 min.

3. Stir in chopped **garlic**, **ginger**, **lemongrass** and **red chili** (if using). Add ground **coriander**, **cumin**, **paprika**, **turmeric**, **cinnamon**, **cardamom**, and **bay leaves**. Fry, stirring constantly until richly aromatic, 2–3 min.

4. Add chopped **green beans**, **pineapple**, **tomato**, and **apricots**. Cook partially covered, stirring regularly, until tomatoes fall apart, 4–6 min.

5. Gradually stir in **coconut milk**. Bring to simmer, reduce heat to medium low. Cook until vegetables are mostly soft, about 7–10 min, stirring in **water** gradually as needed. Remove and discard whole spices.

6. Stir in **lime juice** and **salt**. Stir in **peanuts**, or save for garnish. Cover until ready to serve.

7. Garnish with chopped, fresh **basil** or **parsley**. Serve with rice.

**Variations:**
**Soy chunks**: Soak 1 cup (80 g) large soy chunks in hot water for 20 min. Drain and press out extra water. Fry soaked chunks in place of, or with tofu. Adjust lime juice and salt if needed. **Vegetables**: Substitute or add chopped broccoli, cauliflower, potatoes, eggplant (aubergine), bamboo shoots, etc. after adding spices.

# Ful Medames
## North African spicy bean dip

serves 2 / time 30 min +

**2 cups (325 g) fava beans / broad beans** (cooked)
or **1 cup (175 g) fava beans / broad beans** (dried)
**1 small (70 g) tomato** chopped
**1 small (65 g) onion** finely chopped
**2–3 cloves garlic** finely chopped
**3 Tbs olive oil** more for garnish
**1 tsp paprika** ground
**1/2 tsp black pepper** ground
**1/4 tsp cumin** ground
**1/4 tsp coriander** ground
**3/4 tsp salt**
**1/2 cup (120 ml) water** more as needed
**1 Tbs lemon juice** *optional*
**1 green chili pepper** sliced *optional*
**1 baguette** or other **fresh bread**

1. If using dry **fava beans**, soak overnight. Drain and discard water. Boil beans in fresh water (without salt) until soft, 60–90 min (possibly longer). Drain.
2. If using cooked **beans**, drain and rinse.
3. Heat **olive oil** in a medium pot on medium low heat.
4. Add chopped **onion**. Fry, stirring regularly, 2–3 min.
5. Add chopped **garlic**, ground **paprika**, **black pepper**, **cumin**, **coriander**, and **salt**. Fry, stirring constantly, until richly aromatic and onions are soft and browned, 3–5 min.
6. Add cooked **beans** and chopped **tomatoes**. Mix well and mash beans. Cook until tomatoes start to fall apart, 3–5 min.
7. Add **water**. Continue to cook, stirring regularly, adding **water** if needed, to desired thickness, 5–10 min. Stir in **lemon juice** (if using). Remove from heat.
8. Transfer to a bowl or plate. Garnish with sliced **chili** (if using). Drizzle with **olive oil**. Serve with **baguette** or other **fresh bread**.

### Variations:
**Other beans:** Substitute or combine with other beans such as chickpeas or white beans.

# Hummus
## North African & Middle Eastern blended chickpea spread

serves 2 to 3 / time 20 min

**1/2 cup + 1 Tbs (100 g) dried chickpeas**
or **1 1/2 cups (240 g) cooked chickpeas**
**1 tsp baking soda** *optional*
**4 Tbs lemon juice**
**3 Tbs tahini**
**3–4 Tbs olive oil** more as needed
**3–4 Tbs cold water** more as needed
**1 tsp salt**

**1/4 tsp smoked paprika** ground
**small handful fresh parsley** chopped, for garnish

1. If using dried **chickpeas**, rinse and cover with water and soak overnight. Drain and discard soaking water. Bring a large pot of water to boil and cook chickpeas until soft, 60–90 min.
2. Rinse and drain cooked **chickpeas**.
3. Transfer chickpeas to a bowl and cover with hot water. Stir in **baking soda**. Let sit 10 min. Drain and discard water. Rinse chickpeas under cold water and rub them with your fingers to remove (and discard) the skins as best as you can. (You can omit this step, but if you remove the skins, you'll be rewarded with smoother, creamier hummus.)
4. Add skinned chickpeas, **lemon juice**, **tahini**, **olive oil**, and **salt** to a blender or food processor. Pulse several times and then blend at increasing speed, stopping often to scrape down the sides with a spatula. Continue to blend until very smooth, gradually adding cold **water** as needed, 2–3 min.
5. Transfer to a bowl or spread across a plate and top with a drizzle of **olive oil**, **smoked paprika**, and chopped **fresh parsley**.
6. Serve with fresh pita or other bread.

**Variations:**
**Garlic**: Add 1–2 cloves fresh or roasted garlic. **Green**: Blend with a handful of fresh parsley and 1–2 cloves garlic. **Red**: Add 1/2 cup (30 g) chopped sun-dried tomatoes or roasted red peppers. **Olive**: Add 1/4 cup (30 g) green or black olives. For all variations, adjust lemon juice and salt as needed.

# Buka
## Nigerian stew with soy chunks & mushrooms

serves 3 to 4 / time 45 min

**2 cups (90 g) large soy chunks** (TVP)
**2 cups (480 ml) water**
**6 large (180 g) mushrooms** sliced
**1/2 large (75 g) red pepper** chopped
**7–8 small (320 g) plum tomatoes**
**1 medium (90 g) onion**
**1 in (3 cm) fresh ginger** chopped
**1 small red chili** chopped *optional*
**1 cup (240 ml) water** more as needed

**3 Tbs vegetable oil**
**1 Tbs coconut oil**
**1/2 tsp coriander** ground
**1/2 tsp cumin** ground
**1 1/2 tsp paprika** ground
**1/2 tsp turmeric** ground
**2 bay leaves**
**2 Tbs tomato paste**
**2 sprigs fresh thyme** chopped
**1 1/2 tsp salt**
**handful fresh parsley** chopped

1. Bring 2 cups (480 ml) **water** to boil in a medium pot. Stir in **soy chunks** (TVP). Remove from heat. Cover and let sit 10 min.
2. In a blender or food processor, blend chopped **red pepper**, **tomatoes**, **onion**, **ginger**, and **red chili** with 1 cup (240 ml) **water** until smooth.
3. Drain soy chunks, discard water. Press to release extra liquid. If desired, cut or tear larger pieces.
4. Heat **vegetable oil** and **coconut oil** in a large pot or wok on medium high heat.
5. Add drained soy chunks. Fry until chunks are browned and lightly scorched, stirring often, 5–8 min.
6. Stir in ground **coriander**, **cumin**, **paprika**, **turmeric**, and **bay leaves**. Continue to fry until richly aromatic, stirring constantly, 1–2 min.
7. Add sliced **mushrooms** and **tomato paste**. Mix well.
8. Add blended tomatoes. Bring to boil. Reduce heat to low. Simmer, partially covered, until sauce thickens and turns dark red, stirring often, 15–20 min. Gradually stir in more water if needed.
9. Stir in chopped **thyme**, **salt**, and most of the chopped **parsley**, saving some for garnish.
10. Continue simmering on low, stirring occasionally, adding water if needed, until stew is desired consistency, another 7–10 min. Remove from heat.
11. Garnish with remaining chopped **parsley** and serve with Jollof rice (page 168) or plain steamed rice.

### Variations:
**Seitan**: Substitute 7 oz (200 g) chopped seitan for soaked soy chunks. (Do not soak seitan.)

# Jollof
## Senegalese seasoned rice

serves 2 to 3 / time 30 min

**1 cup (185 g) jasmine** or **basmati rice**
**1 medium (100 g) yellow onion** chopped
**2 cloves garlic** finely chopped
**1/2 in (1 cm) fresh ginger** finely chopped

**2 Tbs vegetable oil**
**1/4 tsp cumin** ground
**1/2 tsp coriander** ground
**1/4 tsp black pepper**
**1/2 tsp paprika** ground
**1/2 tsp turmeric** ground
**2 bay leaves**
**1 sprig fresh thyme** or **1/2 tsp dried thyme**
**2 Tbs tomato paste**
**1/2 tsp salt**
**2 cups (480 ml) water**
**small handful fresh parsley** chopped

1. Rinse and drain **rice** thoroughly.
2. Heat **oil** in a medium pot on medium high heat. Add chopped **onion**, **garlic**, and **ginger**. Fry, stirring constantly, until onions start to soften, 3-5 min.
3. Stir in ground **cumin**, **coriander**, **black pepper**, and **paprika**. Fry, stirring constantly, until richly aromatic, 1–2 min.
4. Add drained rice, ground **turmeric**, **bay leaves**, **thyme**, **tomato paste**, and **salt**. Mix well.
5. Add **water** and stir well. Bring to low boil and reduce to low heat. Cover and cook until rice is mostly cooked and water is absorbed, 12–15 min. Remove from heat. Remove bay leaves and thyme sprig.
6. Gently mix chopped fresh **parsley** into cooked rice.
7. Cover and let sit 10–15 min before serving.

# EUROPE

# EUROPE

### End of the World
### Finisterre, Spain. 07/2019

Extended journeys have always excited me. Some travel to unwind and indulge in comforts. I prefer bold challenges, diving into other cultures, connecting with real people, and sharing experiences with other ambitious eccentrics. I seek to push boundaries and definitions, to find ways to inspire and contribute to the wonder of this world.

I'm not opposed to relaxing; I just think it's best enjoyed after some effort. I don't need an excuse to get a gelato or a cold drink, nor a treat or sweet, but they're infinitely more fun if I've journeyed to get them somewhere special. It just makes sense that arriving somewhere after days or weeks on foot is vastly more powerful than getting there an easier way.

Rising before dawn and immersing myself in nature and new environments, eating new foods with other folks, arriving in a different town or village almost every day, going to bed exhausted yet excited for the next day – that's truly traveling. That's why I flew to Madrid, took a sleeper train to Sarria, met up with Bram, and set out on the final, five-day, 115 km stretch of the Camino Frances towards the shrine of St. James with scallop shells strung on our backpacks.

It was awesome to arrive on foot at the cathedral in Santiago de Compostela. I'd dreamt of doing so for years. Sure, I can't really compare my camino to that of pilgrims, including my companion, who had been on their way for weeks – or even months. I just know my Way.

We coalesced together in the shadow of the cathedral. The energy was intense. The gelato wasn't bad either.

But the long walk wasn't over. We went three days further; together, then alone. The path curved and started a long, gradual descent. Above the trees, on the horizon a band of deep blue came into view. At first, I thought it was the sky. Then the realization struck with force – it was the Atlantic ocean. Finisterre – The End of the World!

I did as pilgrims have done for centuries. I climbed down the rocks, stripped off my clothes and swam in the sea.

### Caffè Doppio
### Procida, Italy. 07/2007

*"Buona sera! Quattro melanzane... e molti pomodori piccoli, per favore."*

The man chose four aubergines and a bunch of small tomatoes. He weighed them on a scale and called out the price. I passed him a few notes and he counted the change back to me. Every syllable was mesmerizing – the song of an exchange in a language not my own. I briefly considered buying some more, just for an encore.

But then I thanked him, slipped the vegetables into my bag, and slung it over my shoulder. I strolled out of the shop and approached the Vespa. On the second kick, the engine sputtered out a few puffs of old school two-stroke smoke and began to purr. I straddled the scooter and lunged forward, releasing the rusty stand. It swung up and clunk into driving position.

Seagulls squawked as they flapped and drifted in lazy circles over the roofs of colorful dwellings packed tightly on the island's sloped hillside. The evanescing wake of the recently departed ferry bound back to Naples splashed rhythmically on the pillars and stones of the marina. At a café, cups and glasses clinked as the server collected them onto a tray. Inside, a portafilter slammed down like a gavel, casting a spent espresso puck into the bin. The grinder clicked and whirred, refilling the basket, and the barista locked it into place. She flipped the machine's switch and started the next pour.

My motorini continued to idle beneath me. I turned and withdrew the key. The engine rattled to a stop. I pressed the stand down with my heel, slid off the seat, and walked into the café.

There was time for another double before climbing the cobblestone drive to the kitchen to make dinner.

## Metal Concert for Three
## Novi Sad, Serbia. 06/2019

On our way back to our mini apartment just around the corner from the old town square the sky went dark and an intense thunderstorm began. We were pelted with pouring rain as we made a mad dash, splashing through the curvy, cobblestoned streets of Stari Grad. By the time we got to the door of our modest rental, we were thoroughly soaked.

Julia went off to take a shower. Kolja and I dried ourselves with a vintage bath towel emblazoned with the crest of a presumably extinct Soviet-era Serbian hotel. We changed into dry clothes, and sat cross-legged on the rug. We unwrapped a bag of snacks from the local bakery. Julia came out of the shower, dressed herself for bed, and laid down with a book.

The tall windows were partially open to the refreshing breeze, and the half-drawn curtains danced around while lightening occasionally flashed in the distance.

"I'm bored, Dad." my six-year-old son declared. "Mmm, what?" I said, as I chewed the last bites of potato-filled börek. It wasn't the chewing that made it difficult to hear. Rain was slapping the terracotta roof tiles again, and a rumble of thunder had drowned out his words.

"I'm totally bored," he said. He brushed a few pastry crumbs off his face. They fell to the floor and he glanced briefly at them, then back at me. Suddenly, the distorted squeal of electric guitar feedback tore through the room. It sounded like it was coming from the kitchen – which didn't make any sense. A double bass drum line began to echo through the courtyard, and I realized either a band was warming up in the flat next door, or something was happening on the stage we'd seen opposite the towering neo-Gothic cathedral on the square.

"Let's go check out the show," I suggested. He'd traveled to over 20 countries with us in the last five and a half years, been to Scottish and Swedish weddings, Mexican fiestas, Burmese birthday parties, and South Indian dance festivals. But he'd never been to a heavy metal concert. It took a few minutes to convince him to put his wet shoes on and come with me downstairs. By then, the band's sound check was over, and the rain had ended. We emerged from the door and I saw the moon through the thinning clouds.

At the square there was no crowd. Just puddles of water, and a lone woman standing close to the stage. She had charcoal hair and an impressive display of eye makeup. She nodded at us and turned back around.

Mist erupted from fog machines on either side of the platform, illuminated by pulses of purple light. Two guitarists and a bass player casually stepped through the mist. They began to work their instruments. Hard, repetitive riffs and deep chords punctuated by high notes burst from the amplifier stacks. The drummer went into a blur of motion. Another figure emerged clenching a microphone with both hands. He unleashed a series of bellows and melodic screams. The words might've been Serbian – but also might have been Norwegian or French, or even English. Did it matter?

My son looked up at me. He was smiling.

## Fool in the Fjords
### Ullensvang, Norway. 07/2017

"I'm going this way," he said, pointing straight ahead. It was, after all, a continuation of the well-trodden trail we'd been on for the last hour. But it didn't feel right to me. I was convinced that to reach our destination, the one church village of Lofthus, we needed to turn left here and descend a minor trail through the forest of old pines. We were exhausted and our nerves shot after almost 10 hours of trekking, much of it in the rain.

Ominously overcast and early, we'd set out after a simple breakfast at the Stavali mountain lodge, the only real shelter in this remote region of the Hardangervidda. Theoretically, we could have frozen our asses off and slept in one of a few dilapidated rock forts that looked like stone igloos – and reminded me of the crumbling, overgrown meditation huts at a Rishikesh ashram.

But the red lodge offered use of an outdoor, wood-fired hot tub with utterly unbelievable Norwegian mountain plateau views. Eighty bucks each was a steep price for a night in a shared dormitory room, but I won't lie – that alpine hot tub and warm bunk were worth every cent and every step.

I'd known today would be more demanding, but really hadn't expected a few things. Like lots of rain, fields of snow and ice, countless creek crossings with no bridges, and very limited trail marking and signposts. I hadn't brought my boots for this trek because my robust trail shoes had worked out perfectly for a short three day Himalayan hike in Nepal just a few months before. But I'd employed a sherpa on that trip – who knew the trails by heart, and the weather was fantastic. It also didn't involve glaciers and knee-deep icy water.

Suffice to say, by the third or fourth time I'd slipped and fallen on wet stones or had to take off my shoes, roll up my trousers, and wade barefoot through freezing streams, I felt humbled by nature and very aware of my overconfidence.

So rather than going off on my own, I opted to stay together. Maybe I was wrong about the navigation – just as I had been about footwear. We carried on in silence for another hour, another rainstorm. Eventually the trees thinned out, the path joined a long, winding dirt road, and the coast came into view. The twilight glistened on the water framed by the jagged, mountainous fjords. We reached a series of cherry orchards and a few homes. It was the first time we'd seen an actual street since we'd left Kinsarvik, the viking settlement where the trek had begun a couple days ago. Wherever we were, there were no places to stay here. We'd been trekking now for almost twelve hours. Pretty soon we'd be knocking on doors and begging for blankets, a floor to sleep on, and a meal beyond dried fruit, mixed nuts, and tofu jerky.

Another half hour further, a man at a workshop told us we were close to the Ullensvang Gjestheim. The guesthouse in Lofthus was indeed only another fifteen minutes up the road – just beyond a minor trail that emerged from a steep hillside forest of old pines.

# Mâche aux Pommes
## field greens with apples & chickpea ginger parsley dressing

serves 3 to 4 / time 20 min

**4 cups (100 g) field greens**
**1 large (200 g) apple** thinly sliced
**1/4 cup (30 g) sunflower seeds**
**2 tsp olive oil**
**1/4 tsp black pepper** ground
**1/8 tsp sea salt**

### chickpea ginger parsley dressing:
**1/2 cup (85 g) cooked chickpeas**
**1 in (3 cm) fresh ginger** chopped
**1/2 cup (10 g) fresh parsley** chopped
**2 Tbs olive oil**
**2 Tbs lemon juice**
**2 Tbs agave syrup**
**2–3 Tbs water**
**1/4 tsp black pepper** ground
**1/4 tsp sea salt** more as needed

1. Blend all **dressing ingredients** in a blender or small food processor until smooth. Add **water** gradually to adjust consistency as needed. Adjust **salt** to taste. Cover and chill while preparing apples and greens.
2. Wash **field greens** and trim ends as needed. Dry them and arrange on plates or in a large bowl.
3. Heat 2 tsp **olive oil** in a medium saucepan on medium heat. Add sliced **apple** and sprinkle with ground **black pepper**, and **salt**. Sear slices on both sides, turning occasionally, until soft, browned and moderately scorched, 4–6 min. Remove from heat.
4. Dry roast **sunflower seeds** in a small pan (with no oil) on medium heat, 3–4 min. Remove from heat.
5. After seared apples have mostly cooled, arrange on field greens.
6. Top with blended dressing and roasted sunflower seeds and serve.

# Borscht
## Russian beet soup

serves 3 to 4 / time 30 min +

**3 medium (350 g) beets** peeled, chopped
**2 medium (200 g) potatoes** peeled, chopped
**1 medium (90 g) carrot** peeled, chopped
**1 small (70 g) onion** chopped
**2 Tbs olive oil**
**1 Tbs apple cider vinegar** or **rice vinegar**
**1 Tbs red wine** *optional*
**3 cups (720 ml) water** more as needed
**1/2 tsp sugar**
**1 tsp sea salt**
**small handful fresh dill** chopped, for garnish
**3–4 Tbs plain soy yogurt** *optional*

1. Heat **olive oil** in a large pot on medium high heat. Add chopped **onion** and fry until soft, 3–5 min.
2. Add chopped **beets**, **potatoes**, and **carrot**. Cook, stirring regularly, until browned, 4–6 min.
3. Stir in **vinegar** and **red wine** (if using). Continue to cook while stirring for another 1–2 min.
4. Add 1 cup (240 ml) **water**. Bring to low boil and reduce heat to medium low. Cook partially covered until vegetables are soft, 9–12 min. Remove from heat.
5. Blend to desired consistency with an immersion blender, or transfer to a blender and blend smooth, adding more **water** as needed. Return blended mixture to large pot, if needed.
6. Stir in another 1 cup (240 ml) **water**, **sugar**, and **salt**. Return to boil. Simmer on low, stirring in remaining **water** (or more) as needed, 4–5 min. Remove from heat and let cool 15–20 min.
7. Serve warm in bowls with a spoonful of **yogurt** and chopped **fresh dill**.

## Variations:
**Other vegetables**: Try adding chopped celery, parsnip, fennel, etc. Cauliflower can be used in place of potato. Adjust salt and water amounts as needed.

# Blintzes
## Russian-Ukrainian crêpes

serves 2 to 3 / time 45 min +

### crêpes:
**1/2 cup (60 g) flour** (all-purpose / type 550)
**1/4 cup (30 g) chickpea flour**
**2 1/2 Tbs corn starch** or **soy flour**
**1/2 tsp salt**
**1 1/4 cup (300 ml) soy milk**
**1/4 cup (60 ml) water**
**vegetable oil** for frying

1. Combine **flour**, **chickpea flour**, **corn starch** (or **soy flour**), and **salt** in a large mixing bowl.
2. Gradually add **soy milk** and **water** to dry ingredients. Whisk until smooth. Cover. Let sit for 30–60 min.
3. Heat a small non-stick frying pan or well-seasoned cast iron pan on medium to medium high heat.
4. Put a few drops of **oil** on the pan and rub it around with a paper towel. (Do this before each blintz.) When a drop of water sizzles and dances on the surface, the pan is ready.
5. Pour enough **batter** onto the hot pan for one thin crêpe, about 1/8 in (3–4 mm) thick. Cook 3–4 min, flip carefully with spatula and cook on other side another 1–2 min. Transfer to a plate. Continue for another 4 or 5 crêpes.

### filling:
**7 oz (200 g) firm tofu** crumbled
**1 cup (50 g) crackers** (e.g. matzo, saltine) crumbled or coarsely ground
**1 Tbs nutritional yeast flakes**
**1/2 tsp sea salt**
**1 Tbs lemon juice**

**1 Tbs margarine**
**5–6 Tbs plain soy yogurt** or **soy sour cream**
**cherry jam** or **blueberry jam**

1. Combine crumbled **tofu** and **crackers**, **nutritional yeast flakes**, **salt**, and **lemon juice** in a bowl. Mix and mash well. Cover and let sit for 10 min.
2. Spoon 2–3 Tbs of filling into the middle of a crêpe. Fold over both sides and then roll or fold up each blintz, using a few drops of water to seal. Transfer to a plate and continue for other blintzes.
3. Heat **margarine** in a small pan on medium heat. Arrange filled blintzes in the pan and partially cover. Fry until lightly crispy, golden brown, and filling is hot, about 5–6 min, turning carefully after 2–3 min.
4. Serve with **soy yogurt** or **sour cream** and **cherry** or **blueberry jam**.

### Variations:
**Nutty**: Substitute 1/2 cup (30 g) ground sunflower seeds, walnuts or almonds for crackers in filling.
**Other fillings**: Try seared apples or pears, fried potatoes, or sautéed vegetables. **Herbs**: Add fresh thyme, rosemary, or Herbes de Provence to filling. **Sweet**: Combine filling ingredients with 1 Tbs sugar.

# Gazpacho
## Spanish cold tomato & cucumber soup

serves 2 to 4 / time 20 min +

**3 thick slices (50 g) baguette** or **bread roll** chopped
**1/2 cup (120 ml) cold water** more as needed
**6–8 medium (500 g) roma tomatoes** chopped
**1 small (125 g) cucumber** peeled, chopped
**1/2 medium (100 g) green pepper** chopped
**1/2 small (35 g) red onion** chopped
**1 clove garlic** chopped *optional*
**2 Tbs sherry vinegar** or **red wine vinegar**
**2 Tbs olive oil** more for garnish
**1 tsp salt**
**1/8 tsp cumin** ground
**1/4 tsp black pepper** ground, more for garnish

1. Put chopped **baguette** or **bread roll** in a bowl and combine with 1/2 cup (120 ml) **cold water**.

2. Add chopped **tomatoes**, **cucumber**, **green pepper**, **onion**, **garlic**, and soaked bread (including water) to a food processor or blender. Pulse several times and then blend coarsely.

3. Add **vinegar**, **olive oil**, **salt**, ground **cumin**, and **black pepper**. Blend at increasing speed until smooth, about 2–3 min, gradually adding slightly more cold water if needed and adjusting vinegar and salt to taste.

4. Cover, transfer to fridge, and chill for 2–4 hours before serving.

5. Pour into bowls or large glasses, garnish with more ground **black pepper** and a drizzle of **olive oil**. Serve with fresh bread or croutons, if desired.

## Variations:
**Fruity:** Blend with 1 1/2 cups (200 g) fresh strawberries or chopped watermelon. Adjust salt as needed. Optionally add 1–2 Tbs lemon or lime juice.

# Carrot Ginger Zucchini Soup
## classic & creamy

serves 4 / time 35 min

**3 medium (300 g) carrots** peeled, chopped
**3 medium (300 g) potatoes** peeled, chopped
**1 medium (250 g) zucchini** chopped
**2 Tbs olive oil**
**1 small red (60 g) onion** chopped
**2 cloves garlic** finely chopped
**1 in (3 cm) fresh ginger** finely chopped
**1 tsp cumin** ground
**1 tsp coriander** ground
**1/8 tsp nutmeg** ground
**1/2 tsp black pepper** ground
**1/2 tsp paprika** ground
**1 Tbs lemon juice**
**1/4 cup (60 ml) white wine** or **water**
**1/2 tsp turmeric** ground
**1 Tbs nutritional yeast flakes** *optional*
**3/4 tsp salt** more as needed
**1 cup (240 ml) soy milk**
**3 cups (720 ml) vegetable broth**
or **3 cups (720 ml) water + 1 Tbs vegetable broth powder**
**fresh herbs** for garnish

1. Heat **oil** in large pot on medium heat. Add chopped **onion, garlic, ginger,** ground **cumin, coriander, nutmeg, black pepper,** and **paprika**. Mix well. Fry until garlic and onions are browned, 2–3 min.

2. Add chopped **carrots, potatoes,** and **zucchini**. Mix well with spices, cook until browned, 3–5 min.

3. Add **lemon juice** and 1/4 cup (60 ml) **white wine** (or **water**). Cook partially covered, stirring often, until all vegetables are soft, 7–10 min. Remove from heat.

4. Transfer to a blender. Add **soy milk** and purée until smooth. (Alternately use an immersion blender.)

5. Return purée to pot on medium heat. Stir in **turmeric** and **nutritional yeast flakes** (if using) and simmer 2–3 min.

6. Stir in 2–3 cups (480–720 ml) **vegetable broth** (or **water** and **broth powder**) gradually, maintaining a gentle boil. Reduce heat to medium low and simmer to desired consistency, another 5–10 min, gradually adding more **broth** or **water** as needed.

7. Continue to cook on medium low heat, reduce to desired consistency. Stir in **salt**, adjusting to taste.

8. Garnish with **fresh herbs** and some ground paprika and black pepper.

9. Serve with bread, croutons, or crackers.

## Variations:
**Vedic**: Replace garlic and onions with 1/8 tsp asafoetida (hing) and 1 tsp black mustard seeds.
**Pumpkin**: Replace carrots and zucchini with chopped pumpkin. **Cashew creamy**: Instead of soy milk, blend with 1 cup (240 ml) water and 2–3 Tbs cashews, ideally soaked for 30 min beforehand.

# Roasted Root Vegetables
## with fresh rosemary & thyme

serves 3 to 4 / time 45 min

**1 large (200 g) sweet potato** peeled, chopped
**2 medium (250 g) beets** peeled, chopped
**1 small (250 g) fennel bulb** chopped
**1 large (200 g) parsnip** chopped
**1 medium (100 g) carrot** peeled, chopped
**1 large (120 g) red onion** chopped
**3 cloves garlic** chopped

**3 Tbs olive oil** more as needed
**2 Tbs balsamic vinegar**
**2 sprigs fresh rosemary** chopped
**1/2 tsp black pepper** ground
**1 tsp sea salt**

**handful fresh thyme** or **parsley** chopped, for garnish
**lemon slices** to serve

1. Preheat oven to 450°F / 230°C / level 8.
2. In a large bowl combine chopped **sweet potato, beets, fennel, parsnip, carrot, onion, garlic, olive oil, balsamic vinegar,** chopped **rosemary,** ground **black pepper,** and **salt.** Mix and toss to combine well and coat all vegetables with the marinade.
3. Spread mixed vegetables evenly on a large oven tray lined with baking paper. Roast in the oven on the middle rack for 25 min.
4. Mix and turn vegetables and drizzle some more **olive oil** on top, if desired. Move tray to the top oven rack and continue to roast until vegetables are scorched and tender, another 15–25 min.
5. Toss with chopped **fresh thyme** or **parsley** and serve with **lemon slices.**

**Variations:**
**Vedic Indian**: Substitute cauliflower or potatoes for any vegetables and lemon juice for vinegar. Omit onion and garlic. Add 1 tsp Garam Masala and 1/2 tsp turmeric. **North African**: Add 1 cup (150 g) cooked chickpeas and 2 tsp ras el hanout or 1 tsp ground coriander, 1/2 tsp cumin, 1/2 tsp paprika, and 1/4 tsp cinnamon.
**Middle Eastern Makali Sandwich**: Spread hummus in a pita and stuff with roasted vegetables.
**Potatoes**: Substitute potatoes for any vegetables. Adjust salt, spices and herbs for all variations.

# Rotkohl
## German stewed red cabbage

serves 4 / time 50 min +

**1/2 medium (400 g) red cabbage** chopped / shredded
**1 large (150 g) apple** cored, chopped

**2 Tbs margarine** or **vegetable oil**
**1/2 medium (45 g) onion** chopped
**3 prunes** (dried plums) chopped
**2 cinnamon sticks**
**1/2 tsp (5–6) cloves** (whole)
**1/2 tsp (4–5) juniper berries**
**2 Tbs sugar**
**1 Tbs apple cider vinegar**
**2 Tbs red wine** *optional*
**3/4 tsp sea salt**
**2 cups (480 ml) water** more as needed

1. Heat **margarine** (or **oil**) in a large pot on medium heat.
2. Add chopped **onion**, **apple**, **prunes**, **cinnamon**, **cloves**, and **juniper berries**. Cook, stirring regularly, until richly aromatic and onions begin to soften, 4–7 min.
3. Stir in **sugar** followed by chopped **red cabbage**, **apple cider vinegar**, and **red wine** (if using). Mix well. Return to simmer, reduce to medium low heat. Cook partly covered, stirring occasionally, 10 min.
4. Add **salt** and **water**. Bring to boil. Cover and simmer on low heat, stirring occasionally, until cabbage is soft, purple, and richly aromatic, 25–45 minutes. Turn off heat and remove whole spices
5. Serve as side dish with German and Austrian dishes, such as Semmelknödel (page 195).

## Variations:
**No prunes**: Substitute raisins or currents for prunes. **Jam**: Rotkohl is traditionally often made with 1–2 Tbs red or black current jam/jelly instead of dried fruit. **No onions**: Simply omit. **Ground spices**: You can also substitute 1/2 tsp ground cinnamon, 1/4 tsp cloves, or 1/4 tsp juniper berries for whole spices.

# Kartoffelpuffer
## German potato pancakes with homemade applesauce

makes 10 to 15 / time 60 min

**potato pancakes:**
 **4–6 large (1 1/2 lbs / 700 g) potatoes** peeled, grated
 **1 large (150 g) onion** finely chopped
 **1/2 cup (60 g) dried bread crumbs**
 **3 Tbs corn starch** or **flour**
 **1/2 tsp black pepper** ground
 **3/4 tsp salt**
 **vegetable oil** for frying

1. Grate **potatoes** with a food processor or a hand grater. Combine with chopped **onion** in a large bowl. Press the mixture down and pour off and discard excess liquid.

2. Add **bread crumbs**, **corn starch** (or **flour**), ground **black pepper**, and **salt**. Mix well. If mixture is too wet and does not stick together, gradually mix in more **corn starch** (or **flour**).

3. Heat **oil** about 1/2 in (1 cm) deep in a frying pan on medium high heat.

4. Wet your hands and form several 3/4 in (2 cm) thick patties and carefully place them in the hot pan.

5. Fry 3 to 5 patties at a time, until deep golden brown, 4–6 min on each side. Do not move or turn them for the first 1–2 min of frying or they may fall apart! As they finish frying, transfer each to a plate lined with paper towels or a dish towel. Continue frying until the batter is finished.

**homemade applesauce:**
 **3 large (500 g) apples** peeled, chopped
 **2/3 cup (160 ml) water** more as needed
 **1 cinnamon stick** or **1/2 tsp cinnamon** ground
 **5–6 cloves** (whole) or **1/4 tsp cloves** ground
 **2 Tbs lemon juice**
 **2 Tbs sugar** optional
 **pinch salt**

1. Bring **water** to boil in a pot on medium low heat.

2. Add chopped **apples**, **cinnamon**, **cloves**, **lemon juice**, **sugar** (if using), and **salt**.

3. Simmer partially covered, stirring regularly, until apples are soft, 10–15 min. Turn off heat. Let cool 15 min.

4. Remove and discard whole spices (if using).

5. Transfer to a blender or food processor. Blend to desired consistency, adding slightly more water if needed. Alternately blend with an immersion blender in the pot.

**Variations:**
**Other vegetables**: Replace up to 1/2 of potatoes with grated sweet potato, carrots, parsnip, zucchini, etc.
**Indian Aloo Tikki style**: Add 1/2 tsp ground cumin, 1/2 tsp coriander, and 1/2 tsp turmeric. Add or substitute 1/4 tsp asafoetida (hing) for chopped onion, adjusting corn starch (or flour) accordingly. Serve with chutney.

# Semmelknödel
## Bavarian bread dumplings

makes 6 / time 45 min

**2 medium bread rolls** or **5–6 slices bread** (about 120 g)
**1 small (70 g) onion** finely chopped
**2 Tbs margarine**
**1 cup (240) ml soy milk**
**3 Tbs corn starch**
**2/3 cup (15 g) fresh parsley** chopped
**3/4 tsp salt**

1.  Heat **margarine** in a small pan on medium heat. Fry **onions** until clear, stirring regularly, 5–7 min.
2.  Cut **bread** into 1/2 in (1 cm) cubes and combine with **soy milk** and **corn starch** in a large bowl.
3.  Add fried onions, chopped **parsley**, and **salt**. Combine well. Batter should stay together in clumps and not be too wet or sticky. Gradually add more **corn starch** or **soy milk** if needed. Cover and let sit 15 min.
4.  Bring a large pot of water to a rolling boil.
5.  Wet hands and form batter into 6 lemon-sized balls.
6.  Carefully add balls to boiling water and cook 15–20 min, stirring lightly occassionally, as for pasta.
7.  Remove and drain dumplings with a slotted spoon, transfer to plates.
8.  Garnish with more chopped **fresh parsley**.
9.  Serve with other German and Austrian dishes, such as Rotkohl (page 191) and Beaner Schnitzel (page 201).

**Variations:**
**No onions**: Omit and just melt margarine and add to bread mix. **Smoked tofu**: Add 3 oz (85 g) diced smoked tofu to batter. **Mushrooms**: Fry 2–3 finely chopped mushrooms along with onions. For all variations, adjust batter with more corn starch or soy milk as needed.

# Gemüseauflauf
## German vegetable casserole with zucchini & potatoes

serves 3 to 4 / time 60 min +

3 large (375 g) **potatoes** peeled, sliced thin
1 large (300 g) **zucchini** sliced thin
1 small (60 g) **red onion** finely chopped
2 cloves **garlic** finely chopped
2 Tbs **olive oil**
2 tsp **dried thyme** or **rosemary**
1/2 tsp **black pepper** ground
1/2 tsp **sea salt**

8 small (65 g) **cherry tomatoes** chopped
3–4 Tbs **fresh bread crumbs**
or 2 Tbs **dried bread crumbs**
1/4 tsp **paprika** ground
**handful fresh parsley** chopped, for garnish

1/3 cup (45 g) **cashews**
7 oz (200 g) **firm tofu** crumbled
2 Tbs **chickpea flour** (besan)
2 Tbs **nutritional yeast flakes**
1 Tbs **tapioca starch**
1 Tbs **corn starch**
1/8 tsp **nutmeg** ground
1/2 tsp **baking powder**
1 tsp **sea salt**
1/2 tsp **kala namak** (black salt) *optional*
3/4 cup (180 ml) **soy milk**
2 Tbs **lemon juice**
1 Tbs **rice vinegar**
1 Tbs **olive oil**
1–2 Tbs **water** more as needed

1. Soak **cashews** in a bowl of hot water for 30 min. Drain and discard water.

2. Heat 2 Tbs **olive oil** in a large pan on medium heat. Add chopped **red onion, garlic**, dried **thyme** (or **rosemary**), and ground **black pepper**. Fry until richly aromatic, 2–3 min.

3. Add sliced **potatoes, zucchini**, and 1/2 tsp **salt**. Fry, stirring often, until potatoes start to soften, 5–7 min. Remove from heat. Cover and set aside.

4. Preheat oven to 400°F / 200°C / level 6.

5. Blend crumbled **tofu**, soaked cashews, **chickpea flour, nutritional yeast flakes, tapioca starch, corn starch**, ground **nutmeg, baking powder**, 1 tsp **salt, kala namak** (if using), **soy milk, lemon juice, rice vinegar,** and 1 Tbs **olive oil** in a blender until smooth and pourable, adding 1–2 Tbs **water** if needed.

6. Grease a medium large (8 x 10 in / 20 x 26 cm) baking dish or casserole dish with olive oil.

7. Arrange a layer of slightly overlapping fried **potato** and **zucchini** slices in baking dish. Pour 1/3 of the blended mixture over them. Repeat for another 2 layers of potato and zucchini and blended mixture.

8. Top with chopped **cherry tomatoes, bread crumbs**, and sprinkled ground **paprika.**

9. Cover with foil and bake until filling until bubbly and vegetables are well cooked, 25–30 min. Remove foil and continue to bake until the top is deep golden brown and crispy, another 10–15 min.

10. Let sit 15–20 min before cutting. Garnish with chopped fresh **parsley** and serve.

## Variations:
**Vedic Indian**: Replace chopped onion and garlic with 1/2 tsp black mustard seeds, 1/2 tsp ground coriander, 1/2 tsp cumin, and 1/8 tsp asafoetida (hing).

# Zwiebelkuchen
## German savory cake with onions & mushrooms

serves 4 / time 60 min +

### crust:

2 tsp dry active yeast
1 tsp sugar
1 cup (240 ml) warm water

3 cups (380 g) **flour** (all-purpose / type 550)
2 tsp sea salt
2–3 Tbs olive oil

1. Whisk **yeast**, **sugar**, and 1/2 cup (120 ml) **water** in a small bowl. Cover and let sit 5–10 min.
2. Combine **flour** and **salt** in a large mixing bowl. While mixing, gradually add yeast water and work in remaining 1/2 cup (120 ml) water and 1 Tbs **olive oil**. Combine well and knead for 1–2 min. Gradually work in another 1–2 Tbs **olive oil** and knead until smooth and rubbery, about 3–5 min.
3. Cover and let rise in a warm place for 1–2 hrs.

### filling:

6 oz (175 g) **firm tofu** crumbled
1/3 cup (45 g) **cashews** and/or **sunflower seeds**
3 Tbs nutritional yeast flakes
2 Tbs chickpea flour
2 Tbs tapioca starch
1 Tbs corn starch
1/2 tsp turmeric ground
1/4 tsp nutmeg ground
1 cup (240 ml) **soy milk** more as needed
3 Tbs lemon juice
1 tsp lemon zest
1 tsp sea salt

### onions & mushrooms:

5 medium (450 g) **red onions** or **leeks** sliced
4 medium (90 g) **mushrooms** chopped
2 Tbs olive oil
1 tsp **smoked paprika** ground
3/4 tsp **black pepper** ground
2–3 sprigs **fresh rosemary** chopped
or **1 tsp dried rosemary**
1/4 tsp sea salt

**handful fresh parsley** chopped

1. Soak **cashews** (and/or **sunflower seeds**) in a bowl of hot water for 30 min. Drain and discard water.
2. Heat **olive oil** in a large pot on medium heat. Add chopped **onions** (or **leeks**). Fry 4–5 min, stirring often.
3. Add chopped **mushrooms**, **paprika**, **black pepper**, **rosemary**, and 1/4 tsp **salt**. Continue to fry 2–3 min.
4. Preheat oven to 400°F / 200°C / level 6.
5. Blend crumbled **tofu**, soaked **cashews** (and/or **sunflower seeds**), **nutritional yeast**, **chickpea flour**, **tapioca starch**, **corn starch**, ground **turmeric**, **nutmeg**, **soy milk**, **lemon juice** and **zest**, and **salt** in a blender until smooth and pourable, adding a bit more soy milk if needed.
6. Grease a large baking tray or baking dish with oil. Knead risen dough a few times and spread or roll out evenly and thinly to fill the pan. Pinch, pull, and turn up edges to form a thick border to contain filling.
7. Spread about 2/3 of fried onions and mushrooms evenly across the crust. Pour blended mixture over it. Arrange the remaining fried onions and mushrooms evenly across the top.
8. Bake until the top and crust are golden brown and a toothpick comes out clean, about 25–45 minutes. Remove from oven. Let cool 15–20 min before cutting.
9. Garnish with chopped **fresh parsley** and ground **black pepper** and serve.

# Beaner Schnitzel
## Austrian-style breaded bean cutlets

makes 5 to 6 / time 60 min

**1 1/2 cups (11 oz / 300 g) white beans** or **chickpeas** (cooked)
**1 cup (120 g) dried bread crumbs** more as needed
**1–2 cloves garlic** finely chopped *optional*
**1/2 cup (120 ml) soy milk** more as needed
**1 Tbs lemon juice**
**1 tsp lemon zest**
**1 tsp dried thyme**
**1/2 tsp black pepper** ground
**3/4 tsp sea salt**
**3 Tbs wheat gluten (seitan) flour** or **flour** (all-purpose)
**2 Tbs corn starch**
**2–3 Tbs vegetable oil**
**paprika** ground, for garnish
**5–6 lemon slices**

1.  In a large bowl, mash cooked **beans** thoroughly with 1/2 cup (60 g) **bread crumbs** and chopped **garlic** (if using).
2.  Add 1/4 cup (60 ml) **soy milk**, **lemon juice**, **lemon zest**, **thyme**, ground **black pepper**, **salt**, **gluten flour** (or **flour**), and **corn starch**. Combine well. Add slightly more bread crumbs or soy milk as needed if the mixture is too wet and sticky or too dry and clumpy.
3.  Pour remaining 1/4 cup (60 ml) **soy milk** in a large bowl.
4.  Spread remaining 1/2 cup (60 g) **bread crumbs** on a plate.
5.  Form 3/4 in (2 cm) thick patties with wet hands.
6.  Heat **oil** in large frying pan on medium heat.
7.  Carefully dip both sides of cutlets in soy milk, then place in bread crumbs to coat each side. Place 2 to 3 breaded cutlets in the hot frying pan.
8.  Fry cutlets for 4–6 min on each side until golden brown. Transfer to a plate.
9.  Sprinkle with ground **paprika**. Serve with **lemon** slices.

# Käsespätzle
## Swiss-German noodles with leeks & cashew cheese sauce

serves 2 / time 45 min +

**cashew cheese sauce:**
- 1/4 cup (30 g) cashews
- 2 Tbs nutritional yeast flakes
- 2 tsp corn starch
- 2 tsp tapioca starch
- 1/4 tsp turmeric ground
- 3/4 tsp sea salt
- 1 Tbs lemon juice
- 1 tsp lemon zest
- 2/3 cup (160 ml) soy milk
- 1/4 cup (60 ml) water more as needed
- 1 Tbs olive oil

**leeks:**
- 1 large (140 g) leek chopped
- 1 Tbs olive oil
- 1/4 tsp black pepper ground
- 1/4 tsp sea salt

fresh parsley chopped, for garnish

1. Soak **cashews** in a bowl of hot water for 30 min. Drain and discard water.
2. Blend soaked cashews, **nutritional yeast flakes**, **corn starch**, **tapioca starch**, **turmeric**, **salt**, **lemon juice**, **lemon zest**, **soy milk**, and **water** in a blender until smooth, adding slightly more water if needed.
3. Heat 1 Tbs **olive oil** in a medium pot on medium heat. Pour in blended mixture. Cook until thickened, stirring constantly, 3–5 min. Remove from heat.
4. Heat 1 Tbs **olive oil** in a small pan on medium heat. Add chopped **leek**, ground **black pepper**, and **salt**. Cook until soft and lightly scorched, 5–7 min. Remove from heat. Cover and set aside.

**spätzle noodles:**
- 2 cups (250 g) flour (all-purpose / type 550) more as needed
- 1/4 cup (35 g) chickpea flour
- 2 Tbs soy flour or corn starch
- 1/2 tsp sea salt
- 3/4 cup (180 ml) soy milk
- 1–2 Tbs olive oil

1. Combine **flour**, **chickpea flour**, **soy flour** or **corn starch**, and **salt** in large mixing bowl.
2. Add **soy milk** to dry ingredients and mix well. Use hands to knead a smooth, soft dough. Add flour if dough is too sticky and moist. Cover and let dough rest for 30–60 min.
3. Bring a large pot of water to a rolling boil on medium high heat.
4. Grate dough through the holes of a large grater onto a plate. Knead more **flour** into dough if you're having trouble. Alternately, roll out dough on a floured cutting board and slice thin noodles with a knife.
5. Add grated or sliced dough to boiling water. Cook noodles in 1 or 2 batches, stirring gently. Drain noodles with a slotted spoon after they rise and float on the surface, 3–4 min. Transfer to a plate.
6. Heat **olive oil** in a large frying pan on medium heat. Add cooked noodles and leeks. Fry, turning regularly, 3–4 min. Pour cheese sauce on noodles. Continue to fry, stirring gently, until browned and crispy, 2–3 min.
7. Serve on plates garnished with chopped fresh **parsley**.

# Tofu Mushroom Stroganoff
## with onions & herbs

serves 2 to 3 / time 30 min

**5 oz (150 g) smoked tofu** cut in strips or cubes
**6 large (160 g) mushrooms** sliced
**1 small (60 g) onion** chopped

**2 Tbs olive oil**
**1/2 tsp black pepper** ground
**2 Tbs red wine**
**2 sprigs fresh rosemary** or **1 tsp dried rosemary**
**1 sprig fresh thyme** or **1/2 tsp dried thyme**
**3/4 cup (180 ml) soy cream**
or **2/3 cup (160 ml) soy milk + 1 Tbs flour**
**3/4 tsp salt**
**small handful fresh parsley** chopped
**2–3 Tbs dried cranberries**

1. Heat **olive oil** in a large pan on medium heat.
2. Add chopped **onion** and ground **black pepper**. Fry until onion softens, 4–5 minutes.
3. Add chopped **smoked tofu** and sliced **mushrooms** and mix well. Fry until tofu is browned, 2–3 min.
4. Add **red wine**, **rosemary**, and **thyme**. Cook partially covered, stirring often, 5 min.
5. Gradually stir in **soy cream** (or **soy milk** whisked with **flour**) and **salt**. Bring to low boil and reduce heat to low. Simmer partially covered, stirring occasionally, 4–5 min. Stir in 1–2 Tbs water if needed. Remove from heat.
6. Stir in (or garnish with) chopped **fresh parsley** and **dried cranberries**.
7. Serve with potatoes, Semmelknödel (page 195), or steamed grains of your choice.

### Variations:
**Tomatoes**: Add 2 chopped plum tomatoes or 3–4 chopped sun-dried tomatoes along with or instead of wine.
**Seitan**: Substitute chopped seitan for tofu and make Seitan Stroganoff.

# Quiche
## French tart with vegetable & tofu filling

serves 3 to 4 / time 70 min +

**pastry crust:**

1 2/3 cup (240 g) **flour** (all-purpose / type 550)
1/2 tsp **baking powder**
1 tsp **sugar**
1/2 tsp **sea salt**

1/3 cup (80 g) **margarine**
2 tsp **apple cider vinegar** or **rice vinegar**
1/3 cup (80 ml) **cold water**

1. Combine **flour, baking powder, sugar,** and **salt** in a large bowl. Mix **vinegar** and **water** in a small bowl.
2. Add **margarine** and mix of vinegar and water to large bowl. Combine well and knead to form a smooth dough, adding slightly more flour or water if needed. Cover dough, set aside for 30–60 min.
3. Grease a medium large (e.g. 10 in / 25 cm round) baking dish.
4. Press and spread dough evenly on bottom and along sides. Poke bottom several times with a fork.

**vegetable & tofu filling:**

1 1/2 cups (160 g) **broccoli** chopped
or other **vegetables** (see Variations)
1–2 cloves **garlic** finely chopped
1/2 cup (60 g) **cashews**
7 oz (200 g) **firm tofu** crumbled
3 Tbs **nutritional yeast flakes**
2 Tbs **chickpea flour** (besan)
1 Tbs **tapioca starch**
1 Tbs **corn starch**

1/2 tsp **turmeric** ground
1/8 tsp **nutmeg** ground
1/2 tsp **black pepper** ground
1/2 tsp **kala namak** (black salt) *optional*
1 tsp **sea salt**
1 cup (240 ml) **soy milk** more as needed
1/4 cup (60 ml) **white wine** or **vegetable broth**
2 Tbs **lemon juice**
2 Tbs **olive oil**

1. Soak **cashews** in a bowl of boiling hot water for 30 min. Drain and discard water.
2. Preheat oven to 400°F / 200°C / level 6.
3. Combine soaked cashews, crumbled **tofu, nutritional yeast flakes, chickpea flour, tapioca starch, corn starch**, ground **turmeric, nutmeg, black pepper, kala namak** (if using), **salt, soy milk, wine** (or **vegetable broth**), **lemon juice**, and 1 Tbs **olive oil** in a blender. Blend on high until smooth and pourable, adding slightly more soy milk if needed.
4. Heat 1 Tbs **olive oil** in a pan on medium heat. Add chopped **garlic**. Fry, stirring constantly, 2–3 min.
5. Add chopped **broccoli** (or other vegetables). Saute lightly, stirring regularly, 3–5 min.
6. Spread sauteed vegetables over prepared crust. Carefully pour blended filling mix evenly over everything.
7. Bake 35–50 min until golden brown on top and a knife or toothpick comes out clean. Remove from oven.
8. Let cool 15–20 min before cutting and serving.

### Variations:
**Quiche aux Champignons**: Use chopped mushrooms and shallots. **Quiche aux Provençale**: Use chopped tomatoes and leeks. **Quiche Florentine**: Use chopped fresh spinach. **Vedic**: Omit garlic. Lightly fry vegetables with 1/2 tsp ground coriander, 1/2 tsp ground cumin, and 1/4 tsp asafoetida (hing).

# Stamppot
## Dutch mashed potatoes with endives & vegan sausage

serves 3 / time 60 min

**5–6 medium (1000 g) potatoes** peeled, chopped
**3 large (300 g) Belgian endives** (witloof / chicory) chopped
**2 large (100 g) shallots** chopped
**5.5 oz (150 g) vegan sausage**

**1 cup (240 ml) soy milk**
**3 Tbs margarine**
**1 1/2 tsp sea salt**

**1–2 Tbs vegetable oil**
**1/2 tsp black pepper** ground
**1/2 tsp smoked paprika** ground
**spring onion greens** or **fresh parsley** chopped, for garnish

1. Cook chopped **potatoes** in a pot of boiling water until soft, 25–30 min. Remove from heat. Drain and discard water.
2. Add **soy milk**, **margarine**, and **salt**. Mix well and mash with a fork or potato masher until smooth. Cover and set aside.
3. Heat **oil** in a frying pan on medium heat. Add chopped **shallots**. Fry until slightly browned and softened, stirring regularly, 3–5 min.
4. Add **vegan sausage** (whole or sliced), ground **black pepper**, **smoked paprika**. Continue to fry, stirring often, until sausage is scorched and shallots are moderately crispy, 4–6 min. (If using tempeh as in the Variation below, increase frying time as needed.) Remove from heat and cover.
5. Stir **endives** into hot mashed potatoes. Mix well.
6. Portion mashed potatoes onto plate or bowls, top with fried sausage and shallots. Garnish with chopped **spring onions** (or **parsley**) and more ground **black pepper** and **smoked paprika**, if desired, and serve.

### Variations:
**Booerenkoolstamppot**: Replace endives with chopped curly kale. Cook kale with shallots before mixing into mashed potatoes. **Dutch-Indonesian**: Instead of vegan sausage, fry chopped smoked tempeh with shallots or spring onions. Adjust spices, and add 1–2 Tbs soy sauce or 3/4 tsp salt and 1–2 tsp lemon juice or rice vinegar at the end. Optionally substitute bok choy or napa cabbage for endives.

# Risotto ai Funghi
## with sun-dried tomatoes & herbs

serves 3 to 4 / time 60 min

**1/2 cup (30 g) sun-dried tomatoes** finely chopped + **3 Tbs hot water**
**1 cup + 1 Tbs (200 g) arborio rice**
**6–8 medium (220 g) mushrooms** sliced
**3 medium (75 g) shallots** finely chopped
**3 cloves garlic** finely chopped
**2 Tbs olive oil**
**2 sprigs fresh rosemary** chopped or **1/2 tsp dried rosemary**
**2 sprigs fresh thyme** chopped or **1/2 tsp dried thyme**
**4–5 fresh sage leaves** chopped or **1/2 tsp dried sage**
**1 tsp black pepper** ground
**1/8 tsp nutmeg** ground
**2 Tbs margarine**
**1/2 cup (120 ml) white wine**
**4 cups (960 ml) hot vegetable broth** or **hot water + 1 Tbs vegetable broth powder**
**1/2 cup (60 g) cashews** coarsely ground or crumbled
**2 Tbs nutritional yeast flakes** *optional*
**1/2 cup (120 ml) soy milk**
**1 tsp sea salt**
**small handful fresh parsley** chopped

1. Soak chopped **sun-dried tomatoes** in a bowl with 3 Tbs hot water for 10 min.
2. Heat 1 Tbs **olive oil** in a large pan on medium high heat. Add chopped **mushrooms**. Mix well.
3. Add **rosemary**, **thyme**, **sage**, ground **black pepper** and **nutmeg**. Fry, stirring constantly, 1–2 min.
4. Stir in chopped **sun-dried tomatoes** with soaking **water**. Sauté until mushrooms are mostly cooked, stirring often, 5–7 min. Remove from heat. Cover and set aside.
5. Heat 1 Tbs **olive oil** and **margarine** in a large pot on medium heat.
6. Add chopped **shallots** and **garlic**. Fry until shallots are soft and browned, stirring regularly, 5–8 min.
7. Stir in **arborio rice**. Mix well to coat with oil. Fry, stirring regularly, 1–2 min.
8. Gradually add **white wine**, stirring constantly. Cook until grains absorb most liquid, 3–5 min.
9. Slowly stir in 2 cups (480 ml) **hot vegetable broth** (or 2 cups **hot water** and **broth powder**). Simmer on medium low heat, stirring regularly, about 10 min.
10. Stir in ground or crumbled **cashews**, **nutritional yeast flakes** (if using), **soy milk**, and **salt**. Mix well.
11. Continue to cook, gradually stirring in small amounts of remaining 2 cups (480 ml) **hot broth** or **water** until rice is cooked soft and sticky, about 30–40 min. Reduce to low heat.
12. Gently stir in cooked mushrooms and herbs. Mix well and remove from heat.
13. Stir in chopped fresh **parsley**. Serve.

## Variations:
**Saffron**: Add 3–5 saffron threads along with final cup of hot broth or water. **Spicy**: Fry 1 sliced red chili along with shallots. **Asparagus**: Substitute asparagus for mushrooms. Adjust cooking time accordingly.

**red sauce:**

5–6 medium (14 oz / 400 g) **plum tomatoes** chopped
1 1/2 cups (360 ml) **water**
1 small (65 g) **red onion** chopped
1–2 cloves **garlic** finely chopped
1 Tbs **olive oil**
1/2 tsp **black pepper** ground
2 tsp **balsamic vinegar**

2 Tbs **tomato paste**
1 tsp **sugar**
3/4 tsp **sea salt**
2 **bay leaves** and/or **fresh sage leaves**
1 sprig **fresh rosemary** chopped
1 sprig **fresh oregano** chopped
handful **fresh basil** chopped

1. Purée chopped **tomatoes** with 1 1/2 cup (360 ml) **water**.
2. Heat **olive oil** in medium pot on medium heat. Add chopped **onion**, **garlic**, and ground **black pepper**. Fry until onions are browned and soft, stirring often, 3–5 min.
3. Add puréed tomatoes, **vinegar**, **tomato paste**, **sugar**, and **salt**. Bring to low boil, reduce heat to low and simmer, stirring often, until sauce begins to thicken and turn deep red, 5–7 min.
4. Add **bay** (or **sage**) **leaves**, **rosemary**, **oregano**, and **basil**. Simmer another 4–5 min on low. Remove from heat. Remove and discard bay leaves.

# Lasagne
## with zucchini & mushrooms

serves 4 / time 60 min

### tofu-nut cheese:

7 oz (200 g) firm tofu crumbled
1/2 cup (60 g) cashews and/or sunflower seeds
1/2 cup (25 g) nutritional yeast flakes
2 Tbs tapioca starch
1 Tbs corn starch
1/4 tsp turmeric ground

1/4 tsp nutmeg ground
3/4 tsp sea salt
1 cup (240 ml) soy milk
1/2 cup (120 ml) water more as needed
3 Tbs lemon juice
1 Tbs olive oil

1. Soak **cashews** and/or **sunflower seeds** in a bowl of boiling hot water for 30 min. Drain and discard water.
2. Combine crumbled **tofu**, soaked **cashews** (and/or **sunflower seeds**), **nutritional yeast flakes**, **tapioca starch**, **corn starch**, ground **turmeric**, **nutmeg**, **salt**, **soy milk**, **water**, **lemon juice**, and **olive oil** in a blender. Blend on high until smooth, adding slightly more water if needed.

### noodles & vegetables:

9 oz (250 g) lasagna noodles (cooked, or use no-boil noodles)
1 large (300 g) zucchini sliced
5–6 large (150 g) mushrooms sliced
8–10 small (75 g) cherry tomatoes sliced

1. Preheat oven to 425°F / 220°C / level 7.
2. Lightly grease a medium large (8 x 10 in / 20 x 26 cm) glass or ceramic casserole dish with oil.
3. Arrange an layer of slightly overlapping cooked **lasagna noodles** across the bottom of the dish.
4. Pour about 1/3 of red sauce over noodles. Next, arrange a layer of sliced **zucchini**, followed by sliced **mushrooms**. Pour and spread about 1/3 of tofu-nut cheese over vegetables.
5. Arrange another layer of overlapping noodles across the cheese, followed by more red sauce, sliced **zucchini**, sliced **mushrooms**, and tofu-nut cheese.
6. Continue with another layer of noodles, and top with remaining red sauce and tofu-nut cheese. Decorate with sliced **cherry tomatoes**.
7. Cover with foil and bake until bubbly, and vegetables and filling are well cooked, 25–30 min. Remove foil and continue to bake until top is golden brown and crispy, another 10–15 min.
8. Remove from oven and let cool and set for about 15–20 min before cutting and serving.

### Variations:

**Dried herbs:** Replace fresh herbs with 1/2 tsp dried for each, if needed. **Vedic Indian:** Replace onions and garlic in red sauce with 1 tsp black mustard seeds, 1/2 tsp ground coriander, 1/2 tsp cumin, 1/2 tsp paprika, and 1/4 tsp asafoetida (hing). Replace mushrooms with spinach, carrots, or more zucchini.

# Champignons farcis au tempeh
## stuffed mushrooms with tomatoes, garlic & herbs

serves 2 / time 50 min

**10–12 medium (300 g) mushrooms**
**3.5 oz (100 g) tempeh** crumbled or finely chopped
**1 small (60 g) tomato** chopped
**1 medium (40 g) shallot** finely chopped
**2–3 cloves garlic** finely chopped

**2 Tbs olive oil** more as needed
**1 Tbs tomato paste**
**1 Tbs soy sauce**
**1 Tbs lemon juice**
**1 tsp Herbes de Provence** or **dried thyme**
**1/2 tsp black pepper** ground
**1/4 cup (60 ml) apple juice** or **water**
**1/2 cup (30 g) fresh bread crumbs** or **1/4 cup (30 g) dried bread crumbs** more as needed
**1 Tbs nutritional yeast flakes** *optional*
**1 tsp sea salt**
**small handful fresh dill** or **fresh parsley** chopped

1. Clean **mushrooms**. Remove and finely chop stems.
2. Heat **olive oil** in a medium pan on medium heat. Fry chopped **shallot** and **garlic** until browned, 2–3 min, stirring constantly.
3. Stir in chopped mushroom stems, crumbled **tempeh,** chopped **tomato, tomato paste, soy sauce, lemon juice, Herbs de Provence** (or **thyme**), and ground **black pepper**. Cook, stirring often, until tomatoes fall apart, 4–6 min.
4. Continue to cook, gradually stirring in **apple juice** (or **water**) until liquid is mostly gone, 3–5 min. Remove from heat.
5. Preheat oven to 425°F / 220°C / gas level 7.
6. In a large bowl, combine cooked tempeh and mushroom stems with **bread crumbs, nutritional yeast flakes** (if using), **salt**, and half of the chopped **dill** or **parsley**. Mix well, adding more bread crumbs if stuffing is too wet, or just a bit of water if too dry.
7. Rub mushroom caps with **olive oil**. Use a spoon to fill and top them generously with stuffing.
8. Arrange stuffed mushrooms in a greased casserole dish. Any remaining stuffing can be formed into small balls and also baked. Drizzle with **olive oil** and sprinkle with **bread crumbs**, if desired.
9. Bake until mushrooms are soft and roasted and tops are crispy and scorched, 25–35 min.
10. Garnish with remaining chopped **fresh dill** or **parsley** and serve.

## Variations:
**Tofu Stuffed Mushrooms:** Substitute crumbled firm tofu for tempeh. **Vedic:** Replace shallot and garlic with 1/2 tsp black mustard seeds, 1/2 tsp each ground cumin and coriander, and 1/4 tsp asafoetida (hing). Fry only 1 min before adding mushrooms stems, tempeh, etc. **Stuffed Peppers & Tomatoes:** Stuff 2–3 pepper halves or 4–5 medium tomatoes with tops and insides removed. Adjust baking time accordingly.

# Töltött Paprika
## stuffed peppers with tomato rice & smoked tofu

serves 4 / time 60 min

- **4 large (750 g) red, green** and/or **yellow peppers**
- **1 small (65 g) onion** finely chopped
- **2 cloves garlic** finely chopped

- **2 Tbs olive oil** more as needed
- **2 tsp coriander** ground
- **1/2 tsp black pepper** ground
- **1 cup (180 g) jasmine rice** or **basmati rice**
- **2 Tbs tomato paste**
- **2 tsp paprika** ground
- **1/2 tsp turmeric** ground
- **1/2 tsp salt**
- **1 3/4 cup (420 ml) water**
- **4 oz (120 g) smoked tofu** chopped or crumbled
- **1/3 cup (80 ml) soy cream** or **soy milk**
- **2 Tbs sunflower seeds** ground
- **2 Tbs nutritional yeast flakes** or **chickpea flour** (besan)
- **1 Tbs lemon juice**
- **2 Tbs fresh bread crumbs** or **1 Tbs dried bread crumbs**
- **small handful fresh parsley** chopped, for garnish

1. Heat **olive oil** in medium pot on medium high heat. Add chopped **onion** and **garlic**. Fry until onion is browned, stirring constantly, 2–3 min.
2. Stir in ground **coriander** and **black pepper** followed by **jasmine** (or **basmati**) **rice**, **tomato paste**, ground **paprika**, **turmeric**, **and salt**. Fry until richly aromatic, stirring constantly, 1–2 min.
3. Stir in **water**. Bring to low boil. Reduce to low heat and cover. Cook until rice is soft and liquid is absorbed, about 15–20 min.
4. Stir in chopped or crumbled **smoked tofu**, **soy cream** (or **soy milk**), ground **sunflower seeds**, **nutritional yeast flakes** or **chickpea flour,** and **lemon juice**. Mix well. Remove from heat and cover.
5. Preheat oven to 425°F / 220°C / gas level 7.
6. Slice **peppers** in half vertically. Scoop out and discard seeds. Rub pepper halves generously with **olive oil**. Pack pepper halves with cooked filling and arrange them in a greased baking or casserole dish.
7. Sprinkle **bread crumbs** generously over them, pat it down a bit, and then drizzle **olive oil** over them.
8. Bake until peppers are roasted, bubbly, and scorched and tops are crispy and deep golden brown, 25–40 min. Remove from oven and let cool for 5–10 min.
9. Garnish with chopped fresh **parsley** and serve.

## Variations:
**Stewed in sauce**: Blend 4–5 medium (300 g) plum tomatoes with 1 1/2 cups (360 ml) water. Add to a large pot with 1 stalk chopped celery, 2 Tbs tomato paste, 1 tsp ground paprika, 3/4 tsp salt, and 2 Tbs olive oil. Simmer 10 min. Pour into a deep casserole dish and place baked stuffed peppers in sauce. Bake for 25–40 min as above.

**Vedic-Indian**: Replace onions and garlic with 1 tsp black mustard seeds, 1 tsp ground cumin, 1 tsp Garam Masala, and 1/4 tsp asafoetida (hing). Fry briefly before adding other spices and rice.

# Spinaci e Cannellini
## spinach & white beans with sun-dried tomatoes & pine nuts

serves 2 to 3 / time 30 min

**2 cups (11 oz / 300 g) cooked white beans** or **northern beans**
**5–6 cups (6 oz / 170 g) fresh spinach** chopped
**1/3 cup (30 g) sun-dried tomatoes** chopped
**3 Tbs pine nuts**
**2 Tbs olive oil**
**1 Tbs lemon juice**
**1 tsp lemon zest**
**2 sprigs fresh thyme** chopped or **1 tsp Herbes de Provence**
**1/4 tsp black pepper** ground
**3/4 tsp sea salt**
**handful fresh parsley** chopped

1. Rinse and drain cooked **white beans** or **northern beans**.
2. Lightly dry roast **pine nuts** in a small pan on medium heat, 3–5 min. Set aside and let cool.
3. Heat **olive oil** in a large pot on medium heat. Add cooked beans and chopped **sun-dried tomatoes**.
4. Add chopped **spinach**. Cover and steam for 6–7 min, stirring occasionally.
5. Stir in roasted **pine nuts**, **lemon juice** and **zest**, **thyme** (or **Herbes de Provence**), ground **black pepper**, and **salt**. Remove from heat.
6. Garnish with chopped fresh **parsley** and serve warm with fresh bread, crackers, or rice.

### Variations:
**Greens**: Substitute chopped fresh kale or collard greens for spinach. Adjust steaming time as needed.
**Beans**: Substitute black-eyed peas, chickpeas, black beans, etc. **Nuts**: Replace pine nuts with sunflower seeds, walnuts, or pecans.

# Vegan Meat Pies
## with lentils & vegetables

makes 6 to 8 mini pies / time 60 min +

### pie crust:

**3 cups (370 g) flour** (all-purpose / type 550)
**3/4 tsp baking powder**
**1 1/2 tsp sugar**
**3/4 tsp sea salt**

**1/2 cup (120 g) margarine**
**1 Tbs apple cider vinegar** or **rice vinegar**
**1/2 cup (120 ml) cold water**
**2–3 Tbs soy milk** for glaze *optional*

1. Combine **flour**, **baking powder**, **sugar,** and **salt** in a large bowl. Mix **vinegar** and **water** in a small bowl.

2. Add **margarine** and mix of vinegar and water to large bowl. Combine well and knead to form a smooth dough, adding slightly more flour or water if needed. Cover and set aside while you make the filling.

### lentil & vegetable filling:

**3 medium (250 g) potatoes** peeled, chopped
**1 large (100 g) carrot** chopped
**1 stalk (70 g) celery** chopped
**1 medium (85 g) onion** finely chopped
**2–3 cloves garlic** finely chopped
**1/2 cup (90 g) brown lentils** (dried)
**2 cups (480 ml) water**
**2 Tbs vegetable oil**
**1/2 tsp paprika** ground
**1/2 tsp black pepper** ground

**1/2 cup (120 ml) red wine** or **white wine**
or **1/2 cup (120 ml) water**
**3–4 medium (40 g) mushrooms** chopped
**3/4 cup (180 ml) soy milk**
**1/2 cup (30 g) fresh bread crumbs**
**3 Tbs nutritional yeast flakes**
or **2 Tbs vegetable broth powder**
**1 Tbs corn starch**
**1 Tbs lemon juice**
**1 1/4 tsp salt**

1. Rinse and drain **lentils**. Bring 2 cups (480 ml) **water** to boil in a small pot. Add lentils, return to boil. Reduce to medium low heat, cover. Cook until soft, about 15 min.

2. Heat **oil** in a large pot on medium heat. Add chopped **onion**, **garlic**, ground **paprika**, and **black pepper**. Fry until onions soften, stirring regularly, 3–5 min.

3. Add 1/2 cup (120 ml) **wine** (or **water**), chopped **potatoes**, **carrot**, and **celery**. Bring to simmer. Reduce to low heat. Cook partially covered, stirring occasionally, 8–10 min.

4. Add chopped **mushrooms** and cooked **lentils**. Increase heat to medium. Cook, partially covered, stirring regularly, 4–5 min.

5. Add **soy milk**, **bread crumbs**, **nutritional yeast flakes** (or **vegetable broth powder**), **corn starch**, **lemon juice**, and **salt**. Mix well. Cook until thickened, stirring often, 3–5 min. Remove from heat.

### How to make and bake the pies:

1. Preheat oven to 400°F / 200°C / level 6. Grease a muffin pan.

2. Knead and flatten or roll out a small ball of dough, 1/4 in (~5 mm) thickness on a floured surface.

3. Evenly pack flattened dough in muffin forms and trim edges. Spoon in a heaping portion of lentil filling.

4. Roll out dough and cut strips for top crust. Make borders and pinch pieces into place. Continue for other pies. If desired, brush pie tops with **soy milk** to glaze.

5. Bake 18–25 min until crusts are golden brown. Remove from oven. Let cool 10 min before serving.

# Domatesli Bulgur Pilavi
## Turkish bulgur pilaf with tomatoes & tofu feta

serves 2 to 3 / time 45 min

**tofu feta:**
- **4 oz (110 g) firm tofu**
- **1 Tbs nutritional yeast flakes**
- **1 Tbs corn starch**
- **1 Tbs lemon juice**
- **2 tsp soy sauce**
- **1–2 Tbs vegetable oil**

1. Cut **tofu** in slabs and wrap in a dish towel. Weight with a cutting board for 15–20 min to remove excess moisture. Unwrap and cut tofu into small cubes
2. Combine **nutritional yeast flakes, corn starch, lemon juice,** and **soy sauce,** in a bowl. Add tofu cubes, mix well, coat all pieces.
3. Heat **oil** in a small frying pan on medium high. Fry battered cubes evenly in batches until golden brown, turning regularly, 4–6 min. Remove, drain, set aside.

**bulgur pilaf:**
- **1 small (100 g) red pepper** chopped
- **12 small (90 g) cherry tomatoes** chopped
- **1 small (60 g) red onion** chopped
- **2 cloves garlic** finely chopped
- **1 cup (185 g) bulgur**
- **3 Tbs olive oil**
- **1/2 tsp black pepper** ground
- **1 Tbs nutritional yeast flakes**
  **or 2 tsp vegetable broth powder**
- **1 tsp paprika** ground
- **1 tsp sea salt**
- **1 2/3 cups (400 ml) water**
- **1 Tbs lemon juice**
- **handful fresh basil** and/or **parsley** chopped

1. Heat **olive oil** in large pot on medium heat. Add chopped **onion, garlic,** and ground **black pepper.** Fry, stirring regularly, until onions soften, 4–5 min.
2. Add chopped **red pepper** and **tomatoes.** Fry, stirring regularly, until tomatoes start to fall apart, 2–3 min.
3. Add **bulgur, nutritional yeast** flakes (or **vegetable broth powder**), ground **paprika,** and **salt.** Mix well.
4. Stir in 1 2/3 cups (400 ml) **water.** Bring to simmer and reduce heat to low. Cover and cook until liquid is mostly absorbed, 10–15 min. Remove from heat.
5. Add fried tofu cubes, **lemon juice,** and chopped **basil** and/or **parsley.** Mix well. Cover and let sit 10 min.
6. Serve garnished with ground **paprika** and more chopped herbs.

**Variations:**
**Other grains:** Couscous and quinoa also work well for this dish. Adjust water and cooking time accordingly.
**Extras:** Add raisins, nuts, olives, and/or cooked chickpeas along with bulgur. Adjust water and salt as needed.

# Grah
## Balkan bean stew

serves 3 to 4 / time 35 min

**2 cups (14 oz / 400 g) white beans** (cooked)
**7 oz (200 g) vegan sausage, seitan,** or **smoked tofu** chopped
**5–8 medium (100 g) mushrooms** chopped
**1 medium (100 g) tomato** chopped
**1 medium (90 g) onion** chopped
**2 cloves garlic** finely chopped

**2 Tbs vegetable oil**
**2 tsp smoked paprika** ground
**1/2 tsp black pepper** ground
**2 bay leaves**
**2 cups (480 ml) water**
**1 Tbs corn starch** or **1 Tbs flour**
**2 Tbs nutritional yeast flakes** or **1 Tbs vegetable broth powder**
**3/4 tsp salt** more as needed

**fresh parsley** chopped, for garnish

1. Heat **oil** in a large pot on medium heat.
2. Add chopped **onion** and **garlic**. Fry, stirring constantly, until onions are browned, 3–4 min.
3. Stir in ground **smoked paprika** and **black pepper**. Continue to fry until onions soften, another 2–3 min.
4. Add chopped **mushrooms**, **tomato**, **vegan sausage** or **seitan** or **smoked tofu**, and **bay leaves**. Mix well. Cook partially covered, stirring often, 2–3 min.
5. Stir in cooked **beans**. Mix well, cook 2–3 min.
6. Stir in 1 cup (240 ml) **water**. Simmer on low 5 min.
7. In a bowl, whisk **corn starch** (or **flour**) and 1/2 cup (120 ml) **water**. Gradually stir into simmering stew. Simmer until thickened, stirring often, 2–3 min.
8. Mix in **nutritional yeast** (or **vegetable broth powder**) and **salt**. Continue to simmer another 10–15 min, gradually stirring in remaining 1/2 cup (120 ml) **water** (or more) as needed. Cover and remove from heat.
9. Adjust salt to taste. Garnish with **parsley** and more sprinkled **paprika**. Serve with bread.

## Variations:
**Vegetables:** Along with (or instead of) mushrooms, add chopped carrots, red pepper, and/or more tomato.

# Gibanica
## Balkan cheese pie

serves 4 / time 60 min

3 medium (300 g) potatoes peeled
3 large (100 g) mushrooms sliced
1/4 cup (30 g) cashews
1/4 cup (30 g) brazil nuts or sunflower seeds
7 oz (200 g) firm tofu crumbled
3 Tbs nutritional yeast flakes
3 Tbs chickpea flour (besan)
2 Tbs tapioca starch
1 Tbs corn starch
1/4 tsp turmeric ground
1/4 tsp nutmeg ground
1/4 tsp black pepper ground
1/4 tsp fenugreek ground *optional*
1/4 tsp kala namak (black salt) *optional*
1 1/4 tsp sea salt

1 cup (240 ml) soy milk more as needed
2 Tbs lemon juice
1 Tbs olive oil

4–6 sheets (11 oz / 300 g) puff pastry
2 Tbs margarine

1. Soak **cashews** and **brazil nuts** (or **sunflower seeds**) in a bowl of boiling hot water for 30 min. Drain and discard water.

2. Cook **potatoes** in a pot of rapidly boiling water until soft, 20–30 min. Drain water and set potatoes aside.

3. Preheat oven to 375°F / 190°C / gas level 5.

4. Combine soaked cashews and brazil nuts (or sunflower seeds), crumbled **tofu**, **nutritional yeast flakes**, **chickpea flour**, **tapioca starch**, **corn starch**, ground **turmeric**, **nutmeg**, **black pepper**, **fenugreek** and **kala namak** (if using), **salt**, **soy milk**, **lemon juice**, and **olive oil** in a blender. Blend on high until smooth and pourable, adding slightly more **soy milk** if needed.

5. Lightly grease a medium-sized (7 x 10 in / 18 x 25 cm) glass or ceramic casserole dish.

6. Melt **margarine** in a small pan on low heat.

7. Roll out and cut **puff pastry** as needed to line the dish. Place a cut pastry sheet in the greased dish. Brush top with melted margarine.

8. Crumble boiled potatoes over the pastry layer. Pour 1/2 of the blended mix over this.

9. Place another layer of pastry and brush with melted margarine.

10. Distribute sliced **mushrooms** evenly over the pastry layer and top with remaining blended mix. Top with a final layer of pastry and brush the top generously with margarine.

11. Transfer to oven and bake until pie has risen, pastry is puffy and golden brown, and the filling is firm and a knife inserted comes out mostly cleanly, 35–50 min.

12. Remove from the oven. Cover and let cool and set for 15–20 minutes before cutting.

### Variations:
**Spinach-Cheese**: Top blended filling with chopped fresh spinach. **Meaty**: Substitute 7 oz (200 g) chopped seitan or vegan sausage for potatoes and mushrooms. Adjust salt and spices as needed.

# Bratäpfel
## baked apples stuffed with dates, figs & walnuts

makes 3 to 4 / time 45 min

**3–4 large apples**
**1/3 cup (35 g) walnuts** chopped
**1/3 cup (40 g) dates** chopped
**1/3 cup (40 g) dried figs** chopped
**2 Tbs orange juice** or **water** more as needed
**3 Tbs sugar**
**1/2 tsp cinnamon** ground

**powdered sugar** for garnish
**fresh mint** chopped, for garnish

1. Blend chopped **walnuts**, **dates**, **fig**, **orange juice**, **sugar**, and **cinnamon** to a smooth paste in a blender or food processor, adding slightly more water or juice if needed.
2. Preheat oven to 400°F / 200°C / gas level 6.
3. Remove the cores from **apples** with a sharp knife. Try to leave the bottom intact.
4. Pack blended paste in the apples. Arrange on a baking tray or pan.
5. Bake until soft, shriveled, and smelling amazing, about 25–35 min.
6. Remove from oven and let cool 10 min before garnishing.
7. Garnish with **powdered sugar** and chopped **fresh mint**.
8. Serve as is, or with vegan ice cream or vanilla custard sauce.

# Apfelstrudel
## Austrian-German apple pastry

makes 6 to 8 slices / time 60 min +

### strudel dough:
**1 1/4 cup (150 g) flour** (all-purpose / type 550) more as needed
**3 Tbs (45 ml) warm water** more as needed
**2 Tbs vegetable oil** more as needed
**1 tsp lemon juice**
**1/8 tsp salt**

1. In a large mixing bowl, combine 3 Tbs (45 ml) **warm water**, 1 Tbs **oil**, **lemon juice**, and **salt**.
2. Add half of the flour and combine well with a wooden spoon. Gradually knead in remaining flour, adding another 1 tsp **oil** after 1–2 min of kneading. Continue to knead well until very smooth, gradually adding small amounts of **oil** (or **water**) if needed, another 7–8 min. If dough is wet or sticky, add flour.
3. Lightly oil a medium-sized bowl. Form dough into a ball and rub it with oil. Place it in the bowl and cover with plastic wrap. Let it rest in a warm place for 1 hr.

### apple & nut filling:
**4 medium (350 g) apples** peeled, cored, finely chopped
**1/3 cup (40 g) almonds** or **walnuts** chopped
**1/3 cup (40 g) raisins**
**1/3 cup (65 g) sugar**
**1 tsp cinnamon** ground
**1/8 tsp nutmeg** ground
**1 Tbs lemon juice**
**2 Tbs bread crumbs**
**2 Tbs margarine**

1. Combine chopped **apples**, **almonds** (or **walnuts**), **raisins, sugar**, ground **cinnamon, nutmeg** and **lemon juice** in a large bowl. Mix well.
2. Preheat oven to 375°F / 190°C / gas level 5. Melt **margarine** in small pan on low heat.
3. Spread some flour on the counter and roll out dough into a large rectangle, as thin as possible (1–2 mm), turning it over often and stretching it carefully. Spread some flour on a clean dish towel and transfer flattened strudel sheet onto it so it will be easier to roll up and move when filled.
4. Brush entire surface of strudel sheet with melted margarine. Spread bread crumbs evenly across the top.
5. Spread apple nut filling evenly over half of the strudel sheet, lengthwise. Fold ends over and roll it up, brushing the pastry with margarine as you go. Carefully transfer strudel to an oven tray lined with baking paper. Transfer to oven and bake until golden brown, 35–45 min. Let cool 20 min before slicing.
6. Cut into 6 to 8 slices. Garnish with powder sugar and serve with vegan ice cream, if desired.

### Variations:
**Quick pastry**: Roll out 1 or 2 large (7 oz / 200 g) sheets of store-bought puff pastry as thin as possible. If using smaller sheets of pastry, roll out two and make two strudels. **Rum raisins**: Soak raisins in 1 Tbs rum before combining with other filling ingredients.

# Lebkuchen
## traditional German Christmas cookies

makes 12 to 14 / time 45 min +

3 Tbs soy flour
2/3 cup (150 g) sugar
3 Tbs apricot or orange marmalade
1/2 cup (120 ml) water
1/4 cup (25 g) dried figs chopped
1/4 cup (25 g) dates chopped
2 tsp orange zest
1 tsp lime zest
2/3 cup (100 g) almonds ground
2/3 cup (100 g) hazelnuts ground

1/3 cup (50 g) flour (all-purpose / type 550)
1/2 tsp vanilla extract or vanilla sugar
1/4 tsp cinnamon ground
1/4 tsp cardamom ground
1/4 tsp cloves ground
1/8 tsp nutmeg ground
1/8 tsp black pepper ground
1/8 tsp sea salt
2 Tbs unsweetened cocoa powder *optional*
12–14 baking wafers (70 mm)

1. Mix **soy flour**, **sugar**, **marmalade**, **water** in a medium bowl. Whisk until mixture is smooth.
2. Chop **dates** and **figs** very finely, preferably with a food processor.
3. In a large bowl, combine ground **almonds** and **hazelnuts**, **flour**, **vanilla**, ground **cinnamon**, **cardamom**, **cloves**, **nutmeg**, **black pepper**, **salt**, and **cocoa** (if using).
4. Add contents of medium bowl, chopped **dates** and **figs**, **orange** and **lime zest**.
   Mix well, form smooth and moist dough. Cover and refrigerate 60 min, or preferably, overnight.
5. Preheat oven to 375°F / 190°C / gas level 5.
6. Line baking tray with baking paper. Top a **baking wafer** with a heaping tablespoon of cookie dough.
   Press to form round and mostly flat cookies. Repeat with rest of dough and wafers. Place well-spaced on tray.
7. No baking wafers? Form round, mostly flattened cookies with a spoon and place directly on baking paper.
8. Bake 12–15 min. Cookies will still be soft and similarly shaped when done. Remove from oven.
   Let cool at least 30 min before decorating.
9. Decorate cooled cookies with icing and garnishes of your choice.

### chocolate icing:
**2 oz (60 g) dark chocolate**

1. Melt **chocolate** in a small pot set into larger pot of hot water.
2. Apply melted chocolate with spoon or brush on cookies. Garnish carefully, let cookies dry.

### plain icing:
**3 Tbs water + 2 Tbs sugar**

1. Stir **water** and **sugar** in a small pot on medium heat until sugar is dissolved. Allow to cool.
2. Pour over cookies with spoon or brush on cooled cookies. Garnish carefully, let cookies dry.

### white icing:
**3 Tbs powdered sugar + 1 Tbs coconut milk or soy cream**

1. Whisk **powdered sugar** and **coconut milk** or **soy cream** in a small bowl. Mix until thick and creamy, adding sugar or liquid as needed.
2. Spread icing over cookies with spoon to fully cover. Garnish carefully, let cookies dry.

### garnishes:
**orange zest**, **almonds**, **hazelnuts**, **candied orange** and **lime peel**

# Tarte au Citron
## French lemon pie

makes 8 slices / time 60 min +

**pie crust:**
> 1 1/4 cup (155 g) **flour** (all-purpose / type 550)
> 3 Tbs (40 g) **sugar**
> 1/4 tsp **baking powder**
> 1/8 tsp **sea salt**
> 1 tsp **apple cider vinegar** or **rice vinegar**
> 2 Tbs **cold water** more as needed
> 1/4 cup (55 g) **cold margarine**

1. Combine **flour**, **sugar**, **baking powder**, and **salt** in a large mixing bowl.
2. Mix **vinegar** and **water** in a small bowl. Add to large mixing bowl with dry ingredients.
3. Add **margarine**. Combine and knead with your hands to form a smooth dough, adding slightly more water or flour as needed. Do not overwork the dough.
4. Form dough into a ball. Cover and transfer to the fridge and chill for 30–60 min.

**lemon filling:**
> 1/4 cup (55 g) **margarine**
> 3.5 oz (100 g) **silken tofu**
> 3 Tbs **corn starch**
> 1/3 cup (80 ml) **lemon juice** (about 2 lemons)
> 2 Tbs **lemon zest**
> 2/3 cup (140 g) **powdered sugar**

1. Melt **margarine** in a pot on low heat.
2. Add **silken tofu**, **corn starch**, and **lemon juice** to a blender and blend smooth. Add to the pot with melted margarine and stir.
3. Stir in **lemon zest** and **powdered sugar**. Simmer on low, stirring constantly, until thickened, 4–5 min. Remove from heat.
4. Preheat oven to 375°F / 190°C / gas level 5.
5. Grease a medium-sized (8 in / 20 cm) round baking dish or cake pan.
6. Press and spread dough evenly on bottom, pinch up along sides. Poke bottom several times with fork. Transfer to oven and pre-bake (empty) crust for 5 min.
7. Remove crust from oven. Pour in thickened filling and spread evenly.
8. Bake until surface is lightly caramelized and crust is golden brown, 25–35 min. Remove from oven and let cool completely.
9. Transfer pie to the fridge and chill for at least 2 hrs before slicing.
10. Garnish with more **powdered sugar** and serve.

# Mandeltorte
## German-Swedish almond pie

makes 12 slices / time 60 min +

**pie crust:**
>    1 2/3 cup (220 g) flour (all-purpose / type 550)
>    1/3 cup (75 g) sugar
>    1 tsp baking powder
>    1/8 tsp salt
>    2 Tbs soy milk more as needed
>    1/2 cup (110 g) cold margarine

1. Combine **flour**, **sugar**, **baking powder**, and **salt** in large bowl. Fold in **margarine** and add **soy milk**.
2. Knead with your hands until dough is even and smooth, adding slightly more soy milk or flour as needed. Do not overwork the dough.
3. Form dough into a ball. Cover and transfer to the fridge to chill for 30–60 min.

**almond filling:**
>    2/3 cup (145 g) margarine
>    2/3 cup (150 g) sugar
>    1/2 tsp vanilla extract or vanilla sugar
>    2 cups (300 g) almonds ground
>    3 Tbs soy cream or soy milk
>    1/4 cup (30 g) soy flour
>    1/2 cup (120 ml) water
>    1 Tbs orange zest
>    1/2 tsp cinnamon ground
>    1/4 tsp nutmeg ground
>    1/4 tsp cardamom

>    **almond pieces** for garnish
>    **powdered sugar** for garnish

1. Melt **margarine** in a large pan on low heat.
2. Add **sugar** and **vanilla**. Stir until dissolved.
3. Add ground **almonds**. Mix well.
4. Add **soy cream** or **soy milk**, **soy flour**, **water**, **orange zest**, ground **cinnamon, nutmeg** and **cardamom**. Mix well.
5. Preheat oven to 375°F / 190°C / gas level 5.
6. Grease a spring-form or large round baking dish / cake pan with margarine or oil. Flatten and spread dough onto bottom and sides evenly. Prick several times with a fork.
7. Scoop the filling into the crust and spread evenly.
8. Bake until surface is lightly caramelized and crust is golden brown, 20–35 min. Remove from oven. Let cool.
9. Garnish with **almond pieces** and **powdered sugar**.

for **Kolja Govinda**

**Thanks for support, love & inspiration**
Julia, Mom, Dad, Adam, Spencer, Ian

**Thank you**
Jens Neuman, Oliver Schmitt, Ingo Rüdiger
Patrick Bolk, Brit Morbitzer (Ventil Verlag)
Joachim Hiller & Uschi Herzer (Kochen ohne Knochen)
Rebecca Hiscott, Oriana Leckert, Christoph Nagel (Kickstarter)
Eric Mirbach (Vegan Good Life / Antagonist), Bernd Drosihn (Tofutown / Viana)
Thomas Reichel (Avesu), Jan Bredack (Veganz), Chris Cooney (The Vegan Zombie)

to all of the cooks & chefs who have inspired and advised me
Abebech Assefa, Abeje Mengesha, Cisco, Demes & Gojje, Molla Kassaw, Zadie
Vaishu, Ekta & Kewalramani family, Atul Lakhar, Monjit Risong, Nazeer & family
Santoshi, Ming Chu, Julia Vazquez, Nisala family, Mettu, Pearly, Pavan, Hakeem & family
Surdham Göb, Sebastian Copien, Nicole Just, Jörg Mayer & Nadine Horn
Terry Hope Romero, Catherine 'Kip' Dorrell, Sarah Kaufmann
Yamuna Devi, Kurma Dasa, Adiraja Dasa

**Special thanks** to
all of my Kickstarter backers, devoted readers & recipe testers in 40+ countries worldwide
Philip Lorijn, Mitsuko Ikeda, Julia Hartmann, Dustin Main, Bram Hubbell, Nicole & Stefan Keller
Oliver Schneidereit & Merle Sengelmann, Maren & Elmar Buschmann, Felix Carl & Tamara Trölsch
Jasmin & Raphael Manck, Alice Schwarz-Filz, Leslie Bocker, Bas & Suzanne Waijers-Klappe, Silke Wilms
Francesco Paolo Maiale, Tonja Nansel, Sarah Goblot, Heather Morgan, Natalie Mayer, Alexander Schrode
Nicole Seggermann, Michael Evans, Rachel Kloter Stansel, Tanja Grath & Clarissa Juse, Gabriele Fischer
Melinda Tyler, Michaela Binder-Maiacher, Rick Jacobson, Jeff Sage Trisoliere, Christin Mattuschka
Eugene Furch, Thorvald Neumann, Daniel Tschinder, Reiner Barczinski, Ryan Full, Milen Spasov
Russ Abdrakhmanov, Kelsey Karin Hawley, Sergey Anikushin, Markus Raupach, Max Thiede
Shawna Maryanovich, Damian Giuseffi, Janne Vollert, William Radkovich
Gwenn Le Roch, Roman Protsiuk, Eljakim Schrijvers

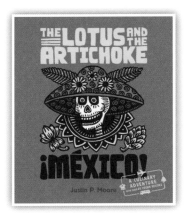

Justin P. Moore
**The Lotus and the Artichoke**
**MÉXICO**
A culinary adventure
with over 60 vegan recipes
128 pages • €14
ISBN 978-3-95575-027-5

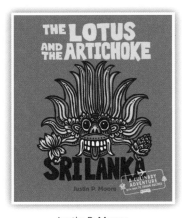

Justin P. Moore
**The Lotus and the Artichoke**
**SRI LANKA**
A culinary adventure
with over 70 vegan recipes
160 pages • €14
ISBN 978-3-95575-047-3

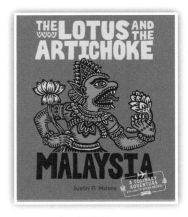

Justin P. Moore
**The Lotus and the Artichoke**
**MALAYSIA**
A culinary adventure
with over 70 vegan recipes
160 pages • €14
ISBN 978-3-95575-064-0

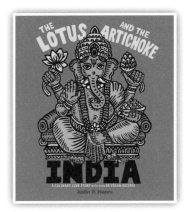

Justin P. Moore
**The Lotus and the Artichoke**
**INDIA**
A culinary love story with
over 90 vegan recipes
192 pages • €18
ISBN 978-3-95575-082-54

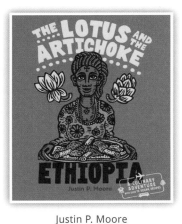

Justin P. Moore
**The Lotus and the Artichoke**
**ETHIOPIA**
A culinary adventure
with over 70 vegan recipes
160 pages • €16
ISBN 978-3-95575-105-0